Hebrew Inscriptions

Hebrew Inscriptions

A CLASSIFIED BIBLIOGRAPHY

Robert W. Suder

SELINSGROVE
SUSQUEHANNA UNIVERSITY PRESS
LONDON AND TORONTO: ASSOCIATED UNIVERSITY PRESSES

Associated University Presses
440 Forsgate Drive
Cranbury, NJ 08512

Associated University Presses
25 Sicilian Avenue
London WC1A 2QH, England

Associated University Presses
2133 Royal Windsor Drive
Unit 1
Mississauga, Ontario
Canada L5J 1K5

Library of Congress Cataloging in Publication Data

Suder, Robert W., 1943–
  Hebrew inscriptions.

  Includes indexes.
  1. Inscriptions, Hebrew—Bibliography. 2. Seals
(Numismatics)—Palestine—Bibliography. 3. Inscriptions,
Semitic—Bibliography. I. Title.
Z7070.S93 1984 [PJ5034.4]   016.4924′17   83-51205
ISBN 0-941664-01-5

Printed in the United States of America

To my father,
who taught me how to search.

Contents

Bibliographic Abbreviations

AA	*Artibus Asiae*
AASOR	*Annual of the American Schools of Oriental Research*
ADAJ	*Annual of the Department of Antiquities of Jordan*
AFO	*Archiv für Orientforschung*
AIUON	*Annali dell'Istituto Orientali di Napoli*
AJA	*American Journal of Archaeology*
AJSL	*American Journal of Semitic Languages and Literatures*
ArOr	*Archiv Orientalni*
Arch	*Archaeology*
ASAE	*Annales du Service des Antiquités de l'Égypte*
AUSS	*Andrews University Seminary Studies*
BA	*Biblical Archeologist*
BAR	*Biblical Archaeology Review*
BASOR	*Bulletin of the American Schools of Oriental Research*
BeO	*Bibbia e Oriente*
Bib	*Biblica*
BibOr	*Biblica et Orientalia*
BIES	*Bulletin of the Israel Exploration Society (= Yediot)*
BIFAO	*Bulletin de l'Institut Français d'Archéologie Orientale du Caire*
BJPES	*Bulletin of the Jewish Exploration Society*
BMB	*Bulletin du Musée de Beyrouth*
BMQ	*British Museum Quarterly*
BN	*Biblische Notizen*
BO	*Bibliotheca Orientalis*
BSa	*Bibliotheca Sacra*
BiTerS	*Bible et Terre Sainte*
BurH	*Buried History*
BZ	*Biblische Zeitschrift*
BZAW	*Beihefte zur ZAW*

9

CBQ	*Catholic Biblical Quarterly*
CHM	*Cahiers d'Histoire Mondiale*
CRAIBL	*Comptes Rendus de l'Académie des Inscriptions et Belles-Lettres*
CT	*Collectanea Theologica*
DLZ	*Deutsche Literaturzeitung*
EPHE	*Annuaire de l'École Pratique des Hautes Études*
Expos. Times	*Expository Times*
EI	*Erets Israel*
FO	*Folia Orientalea*
FuF	*Forschungen und Forschritte*
HThR	*Harvard Theological Review*
HUCA	*Hebrew Union College Annual*
IEJ	*Israel Exploration Journal*
ILN	*Illustrated London News*
JA	*Journal Asiatique*
JANESCU	*Journal of the Ancient Near Eastern Society of Columbia University*
JAOS	*Journal of the American Oriental Society*
JBL	*Journal of Biblical Literature*
JBR	*Journal of Bible and Religion*
JEA	*Journal of Egyptian Archaeology*
JL	*Journal of Linguistics*
JNES	*Journal of Near Eastern Studies*
JPOS	*Journal of the Palestine Oriental Society*
JQR	*Jewish Quarterly Review*
JRAS	*Journal of the Royal Asiatic Society*
JSS	*Journal of Semitic Studies*
JTS	*Journal of Theological Studies*
MGWJ	*Monatschrift für Geschichte und Wissenschaft des Judentums*
MIO	*Mitteilungen des Instituts für Orientforschung*
MNDPV	*Mitteilungen und Nachrichten des Deutschen Palästina-Vereins*
Mus	*Le Muséon*
MUSJ	*Mélanges de l'Université Saint-Joseph*
NESE	*Neue Ephemeris für Semitische Epigraphik* (R. Degen, W. W. Müller, W. Röllig, Wiesbaden, 1972–)
OLP	*Orientalia Lovaniensia Periodica*
OLZ	*Orientalistische Literaturzeitung*
Or	*Orientalia* (Rome)
OrAnt	*Oriens Antiquus*
PEFA	*Palestine Exploration Fund, Annual*
PEFQS	*Palestine Exploration Fund, Quarterly Statement*

PEQ	*Palestine Exploration Quarterly*
PJB	*Palästina-Jahrbuch des Deutschen Evangelischen Instituts für Al-tertumswissenschaft.*
PSBA	*Proceedings of the Society of Biblical Archaeology*
Qad	*Qadmoniyot*
QDAP	*Quarterly of the Department of Antiquities in Palestine*
RA	*Revue d'Assyriologie et d'Archéologie Orientale*
RAO	*Recueil d'Archéologie Orientale*
RB	*Revue Biblique*
Rev Arch	*Revue Archéologique*
REJ	*Revue des Études Juives*
RHR	*Revue de l'Histoire des Religions*
RS	*Revue Sémitique d'Épigraphie et d'Histoire Ancienne*
RSO	*Revista degli Studi Orientali*
Sem	*Semitica*
SMSR	*Studi e Materiali di Storia delle Religioni*
TA	*Tel Aviv*
ThLZ	*Theologische Literaturzeitung*
UF	*Ugarit-Forschungen*
VDI	*Vestnik Drevnej Istorii*
VT	*Vetus Testamentum*
WO	*Die Welt des Orients*
ZA	*Zeitschrift für Assyriologie*
ZAW	*Zeitschrift für die Alttestamentliche Wissenschaft*
ZAS	*Zeitschrift für Ägyptische Sprache und Altertumskunde*
ZDMG	*Zeitschrift der Deutschen Morgenländischen Gesellschaft*
ZDPV	*Zeitschrift des Deutschen Palästina-Vereins*

Introduction

The discovery and analysis of Northwest Semitic inscriptions has played a small but important role in the nineteenth- and twentieth-century interpretation of the ancient Near East. Although inscriptional finds are comparatively rare in the total volume of archaeological activities, these finds are significant for all those disciplines of study which focus on the Near East. Ranging from the clarification of the historical geography of the area to the understanding of the ancient Near Eastern perception of man, inscriptions have provided a remarkable window on the ancient world. It was only natural, then, that the publication of these materials would be of first importance to many disciplines.

Initially, publication was a simple process that consisted of preparing photographs and drawings for collections of inscriptional material. *Corpus Inscriptionum Semiticarum* (Paris, 1881–) represents the high point in this effort. Appearing as a monograph series, CIS simply recorded for the student the corpus of extant inscriptions as they were discovered. Dialectal classification and an integrated archaeological methodology grew as the corpus increased. Diringer's work, *Le iscrizioni antico ebraiche palestinesi* (Florence, 1934) marked the first thorough attempt to gather a corpus of inscriptions according to dialect and area of discovery. Since that time the study of inscriptions has increasingly applied itself to dialect classification and the distinction of linguistic boundaries. Moscati provided a continuation of Diringer's efforts through 1950 in his volume *L'epigrafia ebraica antica* (Rome, 1951). Donner and Röllig, in their monumental work *Kanaanäische und Aramäische Inschriften*, 3 vols. (Wiesbaden, 1966–1969), provided sections of plates, transliteration, notes, and bibliography for each Northwest Semitic dialect. The latest collection of inscriptions, by Gibson, has appeared in volumes appropriate to the dialects included; *Textbook of Syrian Semitic Inscriptions, Vol. I Hebrew and Moabite Inscriptions* (Oxford, 1973), *Vol. II. Aramaic Inscriptions* (Oxford, 1975).

Throughout the history of inscription study, the bibliography of the

13

field has appeared either as an appendage to the corpus of inscriptions, or as an undifferentiated part of Semitic-language bibliography. Donner and Rollig provide a summary bibliography for each inscription, while Gibson contains sparse bibliographic notes. At the other extreme, *A Basic Bibliography for the Study of the Semitic Languages* (Leiden, 1973), edited by J. H. Hospers, includes bibliographic entries on inscriptions, but mixes these entries under the more general categories of "texts" and "literatures."

Because of the progress in the study of Northwest Semitic inscriptions, a bibliography of the inscriptions arranged according to the categories developed by the study seems appropriate. The present bibliography is an attempt to accomplish that end in a limited way. The study focuses primarily on the Hebrew and closely related Ammonite and Moabite inscriptions found in the area encompassed by the ancient Israelite and Judaean Kingdoms and dating from the Late Bronze to the Roman archaeological periods. A final chapter on the Proto-Sinaitic inscriptions was included for the sake of chronological and geographic continuity and completeness. Within these limitations an attempt was made to collect basic bibliographic resources on the publication, classification, and analysis of each inscription. The bibliographic resources were then arranged in the major classifications: Hebrew Inscriptions, Hebrew Seals, Ammonite Inscriptions, Moabite Inscriptions, and Proto-Sinaitic/Proto-Canaanite Inscriptions. The Hebrew Inscriptions were arranged according to site. All bibliographic entries were then numbered sequentially for referencing purposes. Secondary material relating the inscriptions to biblical studies was omitted; the primary target of this study is the inscription itself.

As an aid to the study of the inscriptions, indexes were constructed and appended to the bibliography in order to provide a means for further classification of the individual inscriptions. In the first index (p. 113) the major inscriptions are arranged chronologically from the earliest Proto-Sinaitic inscriptions to the latest Hebrew inscriptions, including the Ammonite and Moabite inscriptions, but excluding seals. This arrangement was not based on any individual school of chronological interpretation; rather, it seeks to provide the broadest possible chronological limits on the inscription. The inscription was then specified by site of discovery and a brief description of the artifact containing the inscription. Finally, the inscription is related to the bibliography entries by means of the bibliographic reference numbers assigned sequentially to each entry in the bibliography. For each inscription the significant bibliography entries (those containing a major report, analysis, or interpretation of the specific inscription) are listed. Secondary works that contain brief mention of the inscription are not cited under the bibliographic reference numbers.

Since the corpus of seals is rather extensive and constitutes an independent area of study, separate indexes (pp. 121–64) were constructed to provide a classification scheme for seals. They are first distinguished according to dialect (Hebrew, Ammonite, Moabite), then according to site, with Hebrew seals of unknown provenance listed in a separate index. Finally, the seals are classified by the name of the owner of the seal, are distinguished as a seal or an impression, and then a broad chronological interpretation is given for each seal. The bibliographic reference numbers indicate works listed in the bibliography that contain a significant report, analysis, or interpretation of the seal. Where the work listed is a work devoted to a large number of seals, the bibliographic reference number will include further direction to that specific part of the work which treats the seal listed in the index. This further direction will be in the form of a page number, a catalogue number (#), a chapter and catalogue number (H8 = Hebrew seal #8), or a plate number (pl.).

Hebrew seals of unknown provenance were placed in a separate index (p. 136) and listed alphabetically according to the name of the owner that appears on the seal. Ammonite and Moabite seals of known and unknown provenance are listed in two separate indexes (p. 157, p. 163). Finally, indexes were constucted for Hebrew royal seals (p. 152) and for inscribed weights and measures (p. 154).

One word of warning regarding these indexes. They are not designed to be exhaustive bibliographic studies of each inscription or seal. Rather, they were developed in order to provide substantial bibliographic entry into the work done on each inscription. Exhaustive bibliographies for each inscription can be developed only on the basis of the researcher's purpose.

Transliteration of the Hebrew alphabet in the indexes is according to the form: 'bgdhwzḥṭyklmns'pṣqrśšt.

The bibliography and indexes represent a comprehensive collection of materials from the early nineteenth century until 1982, classified according to dialect, provenance, and artifact type. The bibliography may be kept current by consulting the periodic bibliographic surveys, "Elenchus Bibliographicus," "Bibliotheca Orientalis," "Internationale Zeitschriftenschau für Bibelwissenschafte und Grenzegebiet," "Old Testament Abstracts," "Kiryat Sepher," and "Bulletin d'Epigraphie Semitique" (J. Teixidor, Syria 44–, 1967–) These periodical summaries have, since the early 1970s, developed categories of bibliographic collection along the general lines emerging from the study of Northwest Semitic inscriptions.

I would like to express my appreciation to the many people who have lent their time and abilities to me during this project. Professors Keith Schoville and Menaham Mansoor of the University of Wisconsin have provided encouragement and counsel at innumerable points along the way. Professor Jacob Myers of the Lutheran Theological Seminary, Gettysburg, has kindly opened his extensive personal library to me in the final stages of the project. Mrs. Ruth Hestrin, Curator of the Iron

Age Section of the Israel Museum, Jerusalem, read and supplied valuable comments on the manuscript and has provided invaluable assistance in obtaining the illustrations for the work. Roberta Griebel, Linda Schluetter, and Kay Stambaugh have lent their expertise in the typing of the manuscript.

If this volume is able to aid students by providing a fingertip summary of resources, and if it is able to save scholars some time in their investigation of the many intriguing problems in Ancient Near Eastern studies, then it will have accomplished its purpose.

Hebrew Inscriptions

PART I
Inscriptions and Seals

The "Pashḥur" Ostracon from Tell Arad. *(Courtesy of the Israel Department of Antiquities and Museums)*

1

Hebrew Inscriptions General Works, Collections, Compendiums

1. Aharoni, Y. "Hebrew Inscriptions from the Period of the Possession of the Land." Lemerhav 5 (1971): 9ff. (Hebrew).
2. Albright, W. F. "Notes on Early Hebrew and Aramaic Epigraphy." JPOS 7 (1926): 75–102.
3. Bardowicz, L. *Studien zur Geschichte der Orthographie des Althebräeschen.* Frankfurt, a.M., 1894.
4. Ben Hayyim, Z. *Selected Canaanite and Hebrew Inscriptions.* Jerusalem, 1964 (Hebrew).
4a. Benzinger, I. *Hebräische Archäologie.* 3d ed. Leipzig, 1927.
5. Bernheimer, C. *Paleografia ebraica.* Florence, 1924.
6. Birnbaum, S. A. *The Hebrew Scripts.* London, 1954–1957; Leiden, 1971.
7. ———. "On the Possibility of Dating Hebrew Inscriptions." PEQ 76 (1944): 213–17.
8. Bliss, F. J., and Macalister, R. A. S. *Excavations in Palestine During the Years 1898–1900.* London, 1902.
9. Clermont-Ganneau, Ch. "Premiers Rapports sur une mission en palestine et en Phénicie enterprise en 1881. . . ." Premier rapport, Jaffa, le 13 juin, 1881.
10. ———. *Recueil d'archéologie orientale.* I: Paris, 1888; II: Paris, 1898.
11. Conder, C. R. "Hebrew Inscriptions." PEFQS 15 (1883): 170–74.

12.   ———. "Inscriptions." PEFQS 17 (1885): 14–17.

13.   Cook, S. A. *The Religion of Ancient Palestine in the Light of Archaeology.* London, 1930.

14.   Cooke, G. A. *A Textbook of North-Semitic Inscriptions.* Oxford, 1903.

15.   *Corpus Inscriptionum Hebraicarum, Enthaltend Orabschriften aus der Krim und Andere Grabund Inschriften in alter Hebräischer Quadratschrift, sowie auch Schriftproben aus Handschriften vom IX–XV Jahrhundert.* Gesammelt und erlautert von D. Chwolson. St. Petersburg, 1882.

15a.   *Corpus Inscriptionum Semiticarum ab Academia Inscriptionum et Litterarum Humaniorum Conditum Atque Digestum.* . . . vol. 1. Paris, 1881– .

16.   Cross, F. M. "The Development of the Jewish Scripts." In G. E. Wright, ed., *The Bible and the Ancient Near East. Essays in Honor of William Foxwell Albright.* London, 1961. 133–202.

17.   ———, and Freedman, D. N. *Early Hebrew Orthography: A Study of the Epigraphic Evidence.* New Haven, Conn., 1952.

18.   Dalman, G. "Studien aus dem Deutschen Evangelischen Institut für Altertumswissenschaft in Jerusalem, 22. Inschriften aus Palästina. A. Hebräische und Aramäische Inschriften." ZDPV 37 (1914): 135–38.

19.   Damski, A. *A Guide to External Sources for the History of Israel In the Period of the Monarchy and the Restoration.* Ramat-Gan, 1971–72 (Hebrew).

20.   Diringer, D. "The Dating of Early Hebrew Inscriptions (The Gezer Tablet and the Samaria Ostraca)." PEQ 75 (1943): 50–54.

21.   ———. "The Early Hebrew Book-Hand." PEQ 82 (1950): 16–24.

22.   ———. "Early Hebrew Script Versus Square Script." In D. Thomas, ed., *Essays and Studies Presented to S. A. Cook.* London, 1950. 35–49.

23.   ———. "Early Hebrew Writing," BA 13 (1950): 74–95.

24.   ———. *Le iscrizioni antico ebraiche palestinesi.* Florence, 1934.

25.   ———. "Note on the Dating of the Early Hebrew Inscriptions." PEQ 77 (1945): 53–54.

26.   ———. "The Palestinian Inscriptions and the Origin of the Alphabet." JAOS 63 (1948): 24–30.

27.   Donner, H., and Röllig, W. *Kanaanäishe und Aramäische Inschriften.* 3 vols. Wiesbaden, 1966–1969.

28.   Driver, S. R. *Notes on the Hebrew Text and the Topography of the Books of Samuel with an Introduction on Hebrew Palaeography.* 2d ed. Oxford, 1913.

29.   Dupont-Sommer, A. "Histoire ancienne de l'Orient." EPHE 4/ 102 (1969–1970): 131–51; EPHE 4/104: 129–42.

30.   Euting, J. "Hebräische Inschriften." AA 7 (1913): 175–79.

31.   Flecker, E. "Hebrew Inscriptions." PEFQS 16 (1884), 82–83.

32.   Frey, J. B. *Corpus Inscriptionum Iudaicarum. Recueil des inscriptions juives qui vont du III siècle avant Jesus-Christ an VIIe siècle de nôtre ère.* . . . Rome, 1936.

33.   Galling, K. *Textbuch zur Geschichte Israels.* Tübingen, 1950.

34.   Gesenius, W. *Geschichte der Hebräischen Sprache und Schrift.* Leipzig, 1815.

35.   Gibson, J. C. L. *Textbook of Syrian Semitic Inscriptions. Vol. I. Hebrew and Moabite Inscriptions.* Oxford, 1973.

35a. Gressman, H. *Altorientalische Texte zum Alten Testament.* Berlin, 1909.

36.   Gross, B. Z. *Inscriptions Reveal.* Tel-Aviv, 1950 (Hebrew).

36a. Hestrin, R; Israeli, Y.; Meshorer, Y.; and Eitan, A., joint eds. *Inscriptions Reveal.* Jerusalem, 1973.

37.   Jepsen, A. "Kleine Bemerkungen zu drei Westsemitischen Inschriften 1. Zkr, 2. Siloe, 3. Lachish II, V and VI," MIO 15 (1969): 1–5.

38.   Klein, S. *Jüdisch-palästinisches Corpus Inscriptionum (Ossuar-, Grab- und Synagogeninschriften).* Hildesheim, 1971.

39.   Lemaire, A. *Inscriptions hébraiques I: les ostraca.* Paris, 1977.

39a. ———. "Notes d'épigraphie nord-ouest sémitique." Sem 30 (1980): 17–32.

40.   ———. *Les ostraca hébreux de l'époque royale israelite.* Ph.D. dissertation, University of Paris, 1973.

41.   Lidzbarski, M. *Altsemitische Texte, II. Althebräishe Inschriften.* Giessen, 1907.

41a. ———. *Ephemeris für Semitische Epigraphik.* 3 vols. Giessen, 1900–1912.

42.   ———. *Handbuch der Nordsemitischen Epigraphik.* 2 vols. Weimar, 1898.

43.   Lipinski, E. "North-West Semitic Inscriptions." OLP 8 (1978): 81–117.

43a. Littmann, E. *Semitic Inscriptions.* London, 1905.

44.   Merx, A. *Documents de paléographie hébraique et arabe, publiés avec sept planches photo-lithographiques.* Leyden, 1894.

45.   Meyer, R. *Hebräische Textbuch zu G. Beer und R. Meyer, Hebräische Grammatik.* Berlin, 1960.

46.   Michaud, H. *Sur la pierre et l'argile; inscriptions hébraiques et Ancien Testament.* Neuchâtel, 1958.

47. Millard, A. R. "Epigraphic Notes, Aramaic and Hebrew." PEQ 110 (1978): 23–26

48. ———. "The Practice of Writing in Ancient Israel." BA 35 (1972): 98–111.

49. ———. " 'Scriptio Continua' in Early Hebrew: Ancient Practice or Modern Surmise?" JSS 15 (1970): 2–15.

50. Moscati, S. *L'epigrafia ebraica antica, 1935–1950.* Rome, 1951.

51. Müller, H. P. "Notizen zu Althebräischen Inschriften." UF 2 (1970): 229, 242.

52. Naveh, J. "Two Aramaic Ostraca from the Persian Period." In B. Uffenheimer, ed., *Bible and Jewish History, Studies Dedicated to the Memory of Jacob Liver,* Tel Aviv, 1972. 184–90. Hebrew version of J. Naveh, *Atiqot* 9–10: 200–201, with revisions.

53. ———. "Canaanite and Hebrew Inscriptions, 1960–64," *Leshonenu* 30 (1966): 65–80.

54. ———. "A Palaeographic Note on the Distribution of the Hebrew Script. HThR 61 (1968): 68–74.

55. ———. "The Scripts of Palestine and Transjordan in the Iron Age." In J. A. Sanders, ed., *Near Eastern Archaeology in the Twentieth Century.* New York, 1970. 277–83.

56. Noth, M. *Die Israelitischen Personennamen im Rahmen der Gemeinsemitischen Namengebung.* Stuttgart, 1928.

57. Oppenheim, M. A. S. *Inschriften aus Syrian, Mesopotamien und Kleinasien, Gesamelt im Jahre 1811. . . .* Leipzig, 1913.

58. Pardee, D. "Literary Sources for the History of Palestine and Syria. II: Hebrew, Moabite, Ammonite, and Edomite Inscriptions." AUSS 17 (1979): 47–69.

59. ———. "An Overview of Ancient Hebrew Epistolography." JBL 97 (1978): 321–46.

60. Prignaud, J. "Notes d'épigraphie hébraique." RB 77 (1970): 50–67.

60a. Pritchard, J. B. ed. *Ancient Near Eastern Texts Relating to the Old Testament.* Princeton, N.J., 1955.

61. *Répertoire d'épigraphie sémitique.* Paris, 1900–1950.

62. Reviv, H. *Inscriptions from the Period of the Monarchy in Israel.* Jerusalem, 1973 (Hebrew).

63. "Responses, Notes, etc." Qad 11 (1978): 34–36 (Hebrew).

63a. Sarfatti, G. B. "Hebrew Inscriptions of the First Temple Period—A Survey and Some Linguistic Comments." *Maarav* 3 (1982): 55–83.

64. Sayce, A. H. *Alte Denkmäler im Lichte neuer Forschungen.* Leipzig, 1886.

65. ———. *Fresh Light from the Ancient Monuments*. 3d ed. London, 1885.

66. ———. "Unpublished Hebrew, Aramaic and Babylonian Inscriptions from Egypt, Jerusalem and Carchemish." JEA 10 (1924): 16–17.

67. Siegel, J. P. "The Evolution of Two Hebrew Scripts." BAR 5 (1979): 28–33.

67a. Simmons, J. *Opgravingen in Palastina*. Roermond-Maaseik, 1935.

68. Taylor, W. R. "Some New Palestinian Inscriptions." BASOR 41 (1931): 27–29.

68a. Thomas, D. *Documents from Old Testament Times*. London, 1958.

69. Torczyner, H. "The Siloam Inscription, the Gezer Calendar and the Ophel Ostracon." BJPES 7 (1939): 4–6.

70. Wahl, T. "How Did the Hebrew Scribe Form His Letters?" JANESCU 3/1 (1970–1971): 8–19.

70a. Warren, Ch., and Conder, C. R. *The Survey of Western Palestine*. London, 1884.

71. Wright, W. *Facsimiles of Manuscripts and Inscriptions, Oriental Series*. "The Palaeographical Society."

72. Yeivin, S. "The Hebreo-Phoenician Writing Signary." *Ariel 25* (1969): 7–18.

Ostracon from the Archive of "Elyashib" from Tell Arad. *(Courtesy of the Israel Department of Antiquities and Museums)*

Hebrew Inscriptions Arranged According to Site of Discovery

ARAD (TELL 'ARAD)

73. Aharoni, Y. *Arad Inscriptions*. Jerusalem, 1975 (Hebrew).
74. ———. "Arad: Its Inscriptions and Temple." BA 31 (1968): 2–32.
75. ———. "The Arad Ostraca." Qad 1 (1968): 101–4 (Hebrew).
76. ———. "Excavations at Tel Arad, Preliminary Report on the Second Season, 1963." IEJ 17 (1967): 233–49.
77. ———. "Hebrew Inscriptions from Tel Arad." BIES 30 (1966): 32–38 (Hebrew).
78. ———. "Hebrew Ostraca from Tel Arad." IEJ 16 (1966): 1–10.
79. ———. "Letter from a Hebrew King?" BAR 6 (1980): 52–56.
80. ———. "The Nehemiah Ostracon from Arad." EI 12 (1975): 72–76.
81. ———. "Three Hebrew Ostraca from Arad." EI 9 (1969): 10–21 (Hebrew); BASOR 197 (1970): 16–42.
82. ———. "Seals of Royal Functionaries from Arad." EI 8 (1967): 101–3 (Hebrew).
83. ———, and Amiran, R. "Excavations at Tel Arad: Preliminary Report on the First Season, 1962." IEJ 14 (1964): 131–47.
84. Brawer, A. J."*ktym* or *kwtym* in the Arad Ostraca," BIES 30 (1966): 258–59 (Hebrew).
85. Cathcart, K. J. "*Trkb qmh* in the Arad Ostracon and Biblical Hebrew *rekeb*, 'Upper Millstone'." VT 19 (1969): 121–23.

85a. Foresti, F. "Characteristic Literary Expressions in the Arad Inscriptions Compared with the Language of the Hebrew Bible." *Ephemerides Carmeliticae* 32 (1981): 327–41.

86. Freedman, D. N. "The Orthography of the Arad Ostraca." IEJ 19 (1969): 52–56.

87. Fritz, V. "Zur Erwähnung des Tempels in einem Ostrakon von Arad." WO 7 (1973): 137–40.

88. Levine, B. A. "Notes on a Hebrew Ostracon from Arad." IEJ 19 (1969): 49–51.

89. Otzen, B. "Noch Einmal das Wort *trkb* auf Einem Arad-ostracon." VT 20 (1970): 239–42.

90. Rainey, A. F. "A Hebrew 'Receipt' from Arad." BASOR 202 (1971): 23–29.

91. ———. "Three Additional Hebrew Ostraca from Tel Arad." TA 4 (1977): 97–102.

91a. Sasson, V. "The Meaning of *whsbt* in the Arad Inscriptions." ZAW 94 (1982): 105–11.

92. Stefaniak, L. W. "Old Hebrew Inscriptions from Tel Arad," FO 11 (1969): 267–77.

93. Van Dyke Parunak, H. "The Orthography of the Arad Ostraca." BASOR 230 (1978): 25–32.

94. Yadin, Y. "The Historical Significance of Inscription 88 from Arad: A Suggestion." IEJ 25 (1976): 9.

95. Yeivin, S. "An Ostracon from Tel Arad Exhibiting a Combination of Two Scripts." JEA 55 (1969): 18–102.

'ARAQ EL-EMIR

96. Budde, K. "Die Inschrift von 'Arak el-Emir." ZDMG 72 (1918): 186–88.

97. Vincent, L. H. "La Date des épigraphes d"Araq el-Émir." JPOS 3 (1923): 55–68.

ASHDOD (AZOTUS)

98. Dothan, M. "Ashdod, Seven Seasons of Excavation." Qad 5 (1972): 2–13 (Hebrew).

AZOR

99. Dothan, M. "An Inscribed Jar from Azor." *Atiqot* 3 (1961): 181–84; BIES 25 (1961): 105–11.

100. ———. "The Excavations at Azor, 1960." BJPES 25 (1959): 224–30.

BAT YAM

101. Peckham, B. "An Inscribed Jar from Bat Yam." IEJ 16 (1966): 11–17.

BEER-SHEBA (TELL ES-SHEBA')

102. Aharoni, Y. *Beer-Sheba I.* Tel Aviv, 1973.
102a. ———. "Notes and News; Tel Beersheba." IEJ 19 (1969): 245–47.

BETH-SHEAN (TELL EL-HUSN, SCYTHOPOLIS)

103. Tzori, N. "A Hebrew Ostracon from Beth-Shean." BIES 25 (1961): 145–46.

BETH-SHEARIM (SHEIKH ABREIQ)

104. Israel Exploration Society. *Beth-Shearim; Report on the Excavations During 1936–1940.* Jerusalem, 1957–).

BETH-SHEMESH (TELL ER-RUMEILEH, 'AIN SHEMS)

105. *Ain Shems Excavations I.* Haverford College Biblical and Kindred Studies, no. 3. Haverford, Pa., 1931.
106. Albright, W. F. "The Beth-Shemesh Tablet in Alphabetic Cuneiform." BASOR 173 (1964): 51–53.
106a. Dussaud, R. "L'Ostracon de Bet Shemesh." Syria 11 (1930): 392f.
107. Grant, E. *Beth Shemesh (Palestine), 1929.* Haverford, Pa., 1930, 206: *Objects Found in City,* n. 131, Apr. 6 stamp.
107a. ———. and Wright, G. E. *Ain Shems Excavations 5.* Haverford, Pa., 1939.
108. ———. "Découvert épigraphique à Beth Šemeš." RB 39 (1930): 401–2.
109. Gray, G. B. "Interpretation of a Scaraboid Bead Seal with Hebrew Inscription." In D. Mackenzie, ed., *Excavations at Ain*

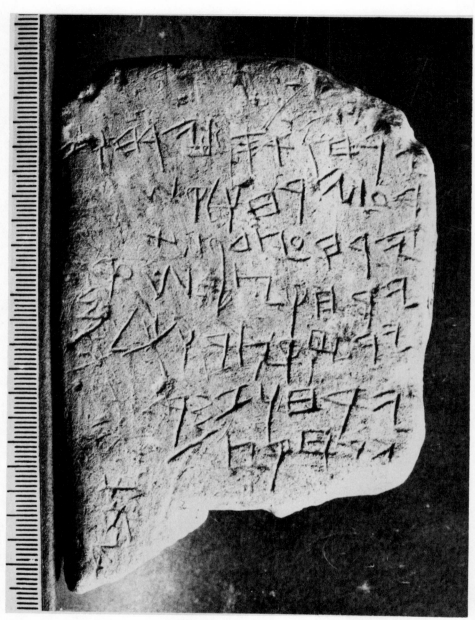

The Gezer Tablet. *(Courtesy of the Istanbul Arkeoloji
Müzeleri Müdürlüğü)*

Shems (Beth-Shemesh). The Tombs of Beth Shemesh (Small Finds from the Chamber of Tomb 8). PEFA 2 (1912–1913): 91–92.

110. Hillers, D. R. "A Reading in the Beth-Shemesh Tablet." BASOR 199 (1970): 66.

111. Mackenzie, D. "The Tombs of Beth Shemesh." PEFA 2 (1912–1913): 40–92.

112. Torrey, C. C. "Brief Communications: Hebrew and Aramaic from Beth Shemesh." JAOS 55 (1935): 307–10.

DAN (TELL EL-QADI)

113. Avigad, N. "An Inscribed Bowl from Dan." PEQ 100 (1968): 42–44.

114. Biran, A. "Tel Dan." BA 37 (1974): 26–51.

ELEPHANTINE (YEB, ASWAN)

115. Greenfield, J. C. 'Le Bain des Brebis.' Another Example and a Query." Or 29 (1960): 98–102.

116. Sukenik, E. L., and Kutscher, Y. "A Passover Ostracon from Elephantine." *Kedem* 1 (1942): 53–56.

GAZA (EL-GHAZZEH)

117. Petrie, W. M. F. *Ancient Gaza.* London, 1931–1934.

GEZER (TELL JEZER, TELL ABU SHUSHEH)

118. Albright, W. F. "The Gezer Calendar." BASOR 92 (1943): 16–26.

119. ———. "The Inscription from Gezer at the School in Jerusalem." BASOR 58 (1935): 28–29.

120. Avigad, N. "Epigraphical Gleanings from Gezer." PEQ 82 (1950): 43–49.

121. Birnbaum, S. "The Dates of the Gezer Tablet and of the Samaria Ostraca." PEQ 74 (1942): 104–8.

122. Bruston, Ch. *Les Inscriptions en Hébreu archaïque et celle d'Eschmounazar.* Paris, 1909. 27–37, 331ff.

123. ———. "Le Prétendu Calendrier de Guézer." *Bulletin de la Société Nationale des Antiquaries de France* (1909), 249ff.

124. Buchman, H. "Zur Kalenderinschrift von Gezer." CT 17 (1936): 520–26.

125. Cassuto, U. "Il calendario di Gezer e il suo valore storico-religioso." SMSR 12 (1936): 107–25.

126. Clermont-Ganneau, Ch. "Deux Inscriptions israélites archäiques de Gézer," RAO 8 (1905): 103–12; RA 11 (1907): 342.

127. ———. "Nouvelle Inscription hébraique et grecque relative à la limite de Gézer." CRAIBL (1898), 686–94; RAO 3 (1900): 116–26

128. Cook, S. A. "Hebrew Inscription from Gezer," PEFQS 35 (1903): 275.

129. ———. "Inscribed Objects from Gezer." PEFQS 36 (1904): 319.

130. ———. "The Inscribed Objects from Gezer." PEFQS 39 (1907): 76ff, 319ff.

131. ———. "The Inscribed Objects from Gezer." PEFQS 40 (1908): 76ff.

132. ———. "Miscellanea." PEFQS 41 (1909): 232ff.

133. ———. "The Old Hebrew Alphabet and the Gezer Tablet." PEFQS 41 (1909): 284–309.

134. Daiches, S. "Notes on the Gezer Calendar and Some Babylonian Parallels." PEFQS 41 (1909): 113–18.

135. Dalman, G. "Notes on the Old Hebrew Calendar-Inscription from Gezer." PEFQS 41 (1909): 118ff.

136. Diringer, D. "The Dating of Early Hebrew Inscriptions, the Gezer Tablet." PEQ 75 (1943): 50–54.

137. Driver, G. R. "Brief Notes." PEQ 77 (1945): 5–9.

138. Ducati, B. "La scrittura." *Bollettino dell' Accademia Italiana di Stenografia* 7 (1931): 21f.

139. Dussaud, R. AFO 5 (1929): 237 (Gezer Calendar).

139a. ———. "Notes." RHR 59 (1909): 138ff.

140. Federlin, T. R. P. "Note." RB 6 (1909): 655.

141. Février, J. G. "Remarques sur le calendrier de Gézer." Sem 1 (1948): 33–41.

142. Garbini, G. "Note sul 'calendrio' di Gezer." AIUON 6 (1954–1956): 123–30.

143. Gobiet, S. "The Gezer Stone." *The Biblical World* 34 (1909): 57–59.

144. Gray, G. B. "The Gezer Inscription." PEFQS 41 (1909): 189–93.

145. ———. "Notes and Queries: 1). The Gezer Calendar Inscription:

A Correction." PEFQS 43 (1911): 161.

146. Gressman, H. "Bemerkungen." ZAW 44 (1924): 364.

147. Halevy, J. "Une Ancienne Inscription hébraique agriculturale de Gézer," RS 17 (1909): 151–53.

148. Honeyman, A. M. "The Syntax of the Gezer Calendar." JRAS (1953), 53–58.

149. Lambert, M. "L'Inscription de Guézer et les chiffres hébreux." REJ 77/153 (1923): 64–66.

150. Lidzbarski, M. "The Calendar Inscription from Gezer." PEFQS 42 (1910): 238.

151. ———. "An Old Hebrew Calendar—Inscription from Gezer." PEFQS 41 (1909): 26–29.

152. ———. "The Old Hebrew Jar-Seals from Gezer." PEFQS 41 (1909): 154.

153. ———. "The Old Hebrew Jar-Seals from Gezer." Records of the Past 6 (1907): 92.

154. ———, Gray, G. B., and Pilcher, E. J. "An Old Hebrew Calendar—Inscription from Gezer." PEFQS 41 (1909): 26–34.

155. Lindblom, J. "Der Sogenannte Bauernkalender von Gezer." Acta Academiae Aboensis. *Humaniora* 8 (1931): 25.

156. Macalister, R. A. S. "Communication." PEFQS 40 (1908): 271f.

157. ———. *The Excavation of Gezer 1902–1905 and 1907–1909.* Vol. 1. London, 1912. 37.

158. ———. *The Excavation of Gezer, II.* London, 1912.

159. ———. "The Gezer Inscription." PEFQS 41 (1909): 189–93.

160. ———. "Inscribed Tablets." PEFQS 41 (1909): 16ff.

161. ———. "Report on the Excavation of Gezer." PEFQS 32 (1900): 316ff.

162. ———. "Report on the Excavation at Gezer." PEFQS 35 (1903): 204.

163. ———. "Report on the Excavation at Gezer." PEFQS 36 (1904): 210ff.

164. ———. "Report on the Excavation at Gezer." PEFQS 40 (1908): 272–90.

165. ———. "Report on the Excavation at Gezer . . . Recent Epigraphic Discoveries." PEFQS 41 (1909): 88–92.

166. ———. "Three Ossuary Inscriptions from Gezer." PEFQS 38 (1906): 123.

167. Marti, K. "Ein Altpalästinensischer Landwirtschaftlicher Kalender." ZAW 29 (1909): 222–29.

168. "Notes and News." PEFQS 41 (1909): 237.

169. Pilcher, E. J. "The Handwriting of the Gezer Tablet." PEFQS 42 (1910): 32–39.

170. ———. "Old Hebrew Signets from Gezer." PEFQS 45 (1913): 145.

171. ———. "Stamped Jar-handle from Gezer." PEFQS 39 (1907): 264; PEFQS 40 (1908): 76.

172. Praetorius, F. "Gezer Inscriptions." ZDMG 74 (1920): 303ff.

173. Rahtjen, B. D. "A Note Concerning the Form of the Gezer Tablet." PEQ 93 (1961): 70–72.

174. Ronzevalle, S. "The Gezer Hebrew Inscription." PEFQS 41 (1909): 107–12.

175. ———. "Notes et études d'archéologie orientale 15. La Tablette hébraique de Gézer. Nouvelles reproductions." MUSJ 5 (1911–1912): 90–104.

176. Segal, J. B. "*yrh* in the Gezer Calendar." JSS 7 (1962): 212–21.

177. Sidersky, D. "Sur un tableau des mois agricoles datant de plusieurs siècles avant nôtre êre." *Bulletin de la Société Nationale d'Agricolture* (1909), 315–17.

178. Talmon, S. "The Gezer Calendar and the Seasonal Cycle of Ancient Canaan." JAOS 83 (1963): 177–87.

179. Taylor, W. R. "The New Gezer Inscription." JPOS 10 (1930): 79–81.

180. ———. "Recent Epigraphic Discoveries in Palestine. A New Gezer Inscription." JPOS 10 (1930): 17.

181. ———. "Some New Palestinian Inscriptions." BASOR 41 (1931): 27–28.

182. Thiersch, H. "Gezer." AA 22 (1909): 347–406.

183. Torczyner, H. "The Siloam Inscription, the Gezer Calendar, and the Ophel Ostracon." BJPES 7 (1939): 4ff.

184. ———. "Towards Understanding the Gezer Tablet." BJPES 13 (1946–47): 1–17 (Hebrew).

185. Vincent, L. H. "Un Calendarier agricole israélite." RB 6 (1909): 243–69.

186. ———. "Gezer Inscriptions." RB 6 (1909): 493–95, 653ff.

187. ———. "Gezer Inscriptions." RB 7 (1910): 158ff., 320, 474, 638.

188. Wirgin, W. "The Calendar Tablet from Gezer." EI 6 (1960): 9–12.

189. Yeivin, S. "The Hebrew Agricultural Calendar." BJPES 3 (1935–36): 120 (Hebrew).

190. Zolli, E. "La tavoletta di Gezer." Bib 27 (1946): 129–31.

The Proto-Sinaitic Ostracon from Gezer. *(Courtesy of the Israel Department of Antiquities and Museums.)* David Harris photo.

GIBEON (EL-JIB)

191. Avigad, N. "Some Notes on the Hebrew Inscriptions from Gibeon." IEJ 9 (1959): 130–33.

192. Cross, F. M. "Epigraphic Notes on Hebrew Documents from the Eighth–Sixth Centuries B.C., III. The Inscribed Jar Handles from Gibeon." BASOR 168 (1962): 18–23.

193. Frick, F. S. "Another Inscribed Jar Handle from el-Jib." BASOR 213 (1974): 46–48.

194. Michaud, H. "Review of James B. Pritchard, *"Hebrew Inscriptions and Stamps from Gibeon, Phila. 1959."* VT 10 (1960): 102–6.

195.   Pritchard, J. B. *Hebrew Inscriptions and Stamps from Gibeon.* Philadelphia, Museum Monographs, University of Pennsylvania, No. 5, 1959.

196.   ———. "The Inscribed Jar Handles from Gibeon." *Akten des XXIV Internationalen Orientalistenkongresses.* Munich, 1957. 213.

197.   ———. "More Inscribed Jar handles from el-Jib." BASOR 160 (1960): 2–6.

Hazor (Tell el-Qedah)

197a. Naveh, J. *"lĕmakbirām* or *lammĕkabbĕdîm?"* EI 15 (1981): 301–2 (Hebrew).

198.   Yadin, Y. *Hazor I.* Jerusalem, 1958.

199.   ———. *Hazor II. An Account of the Second Season of Excavations.* Jerusalem, 1960.

200.   Yeivin, S. "Ostracon Al/382 from Hazor and its Implications." EI 9 (1969): 86–87.

Jericho (Tell es-Sultan)

201.   Albright, W. F. "A Seal Impression from Jericho and the Treasurers of the Second Temple." BASOR 148 (1957): 28–30.

202.   Hachlili, R. "A Jewish Cemetery of the Second Temple Period in Jericho." Qad 12 (1979): 62–66.

203.   Hammond, P. C. "Correspondence (Sealing from Jericho)." PEQ 89 (1957): 145.

204.   ———. "A Note on a Seal Impression from Tell es-Sultan." BASOR 147 (1957): 37–39.

205.   ———. "A Note on Two Seal Impressions from Tell es-Sultan." PEQ 89 (1957): 68–69.

Jerusalem (el-Quds)

206.   Albright, W. F. "The Hebrew Ostrakon." PEFQS 57 (1925): 219.

207.   ———. "Notes and Queries. The Hebrew Ostrakon. Mr. Duncan sends the Following Letter from Prof. Albright." PEFQS 58 (1926): 219.

208.   Amiran, R., and Eitan, A. "Excavations in the Citadel (Migdal David)." Qad 3 (1970): 64–66 (Hebrew).

209.   ———. "Excavations in the Courtyard of the Citadel, Jerusalem, 1968–1969 (Preliminary Report)." IEJ 20 (1970): 9–17.

210.   ———. "Excavations in the Jerusalem Citadel." In Y. Yadin, ed., *Jerusalem Revealed*. New Haven, Conn., 1976. 52–54.

211.   Avigad, N. *Ancient Monuments in the Kidron Valley*. Jerusalem, 1954. (Hebrew).

212.   ———. "Burial Vault of a Nazarite Family on Mount Scopus." IEJ 21 (1971): 185–200; EI 10 (1971): 41–49 (Hebrew); summary in Y. Yadin, ed., *Jerusalem Revealed*. New Haven, Conn., 1976. 66.

213.   ———. "A Depository of Inscribed Ossuaries in the Kidron Valley." IEJ 12 (1962): 1–12.

213a. Avigad, N. "Excavations in the Jewish Quarter of the Old City of Jerusalem, 1971 (Third Preliminary Report)." IEJ 22 (1972): 193–200.

214.   Avi-Yonah, M. *Sefer Yerushalayim*. Jerusalem, 1956 (Hebrew).

215.   Bliss, F. J. "Thirteenth Report on the Excavation at Jerusalem." PEFQS 29 (1897) 180.

216.   Clermont-Ganneau, Ch. "Notes on the Seal Found at Ophel." PEFQS 29 (1897): 304.

217.   Cook, S. A. "Inscribed Hebrew Objects from Ophel." PEFQS 56 (1924): 181ff; PEFQS 57 (1925): 91ff.

218.   Deutsch, E. "Letter of . . . on the Characters Found by Lieutn. Warren at the South-East Angle of the Haram Area." PEFQS 1 (1869): 33–37.

219.   Duncan, J. G. "Report on Excavation of Eastern Hill of Jerusalem." PEFQS 57 (1925): 20, 139; PEFQS 58 (1926): 219.

220.   Greene, J. B. "Some Remarks on the Interpretation of the Impressions on the Vase Handles Found at the Foot of the Temple Wall." PEFQS 13 (1881): 304–11.

221.   Gressmann, H. "Ausgrabungen in der Davidstadt." ZAW 43 (1924): 347.

221a. Kenyon, K. "Excavations in Jerusalem, 1967." PEQ 100 (1968): pl. 36c.

222.   Kutscher, Y. In M. Avi-Yonah, ed., *Sefer Yerushalayim*. Jerusalem, 1956. 349–50 (Inscriptions found in Jerusalem).

222a. Lemaire, A. "Une inscription paléo-hébraïque sur grenade en ivoire." RB 88 (1981): 236–9.

223.   Mayer, L. A. "A Tomb in the Kedron Valley." *Palestine Museum Bulletin* 1 (1924): 56–60.

224.   Mazar, B. "The Archaeological Excavations near the Temple

Mount." In Y. Yadin, ed., *Jerusalem Revealed*. New Haven, Conn., 1976. 25–41.

225. ———. "The Excavations in the Old City of Jerusalem, Preliminary Report of the First Season, 1968." EI 9 (1970): 168ff. (Hebrew); also published as a monograph by the Israel Exploration Society.

226. ———. "The Excavations in the Old City of Jerusalem near the Temple Mount; Preliminary Report of the Second and Third Seasons, 1969–1970." EI 10 (1971): 1–34 (Hebrew).

226a. Mazar, B. "Excavations Near Temple Mount Reveal Splendors of Herodian Jerusalem." BAR 6/4 (1980): 44–59.

227. ———. "Hebrew Inscription from the Temple Area in Jerusalem." Qad 3 (1970): 142–44 (Hebrew).

228. ———. "Jerusalem in the Biblical Period." In Y. Yadin, ed., *Jerusalem Revealed*. New Haven, Conn., 1976. 1–8.

228a. ———. *The Mountain of the Lord*. New York, 1975.

229. Milik, J. T. "Notes d'épigraphie et de topographie de palestineunes, I. L'Ostracon de l'Ophel et la topographie de Jérusalem." RB 66 (1959): 550–53.

229a. Miller, P. D. "El, the Creator of Earth." BASOR 239 (1980): 42–6.

229b. Naveh, J. "A Fragment of an Ancient Hebrew Inscription from the Ophel." IEJ 32 (1982): 195–8.

230. ———. "New Inscriptions on Ossuaries from North Jerusalem." EI 10 (1971): 188–90 (Hebrew).

231. Pilcher, E. J. "Notes on the Ophel Signet. I." PEFQS 29 (1897): 304.

232. ———. "An Old Hebrew Signet from Jerusalem." PEFQS 50 (1918): 93.

233. Prignaud, J. "Un Sceau hébreu de Jérusalem et un ketib du livre d'Esdras." RB 71 (1964): 372–83.

234. Sayce, A. H. "The Jerusalem Sealings on Jarhandles." PEFQS 59 (1927): 216ff.

235. ———. "Note on the Seal Found on Ophel." PEFQS 29 (1897): 181.

236. ———. "Notes on the Ophel Signet, II." PEFQS 29 (1897): 304.

237. ———. "The Phoenician Inscriptions on the Vase-Handles Found at Jerusalem." PEFQS 25 (1893): 31, 240–42.

238. Schwabe, M. "The Greek Inscriptions of Jerusalem." In M. Avi-Yonah, ed. *Sefer Yerushalayim*. Jerusalem, 1956. 358–61 (Hebrew).

239. Scott, R. B. Y. "The Scale Weights from Ophel, 1963–64." PEQ 97 (1965): 128–39.

240. Shiloh, Y. "City of David Excavations 1978." BA 42 (1979): 165–71.

241. ———. and Kaplan, M. "Digging in the City of David." BAR 5 (1979): 36–49.

242. Simons, J. *Jerusalem in the Old Testament*. Leiden, 1952. 75–76, 206–10.

243. Sukenik, Y. "Concerning the Ophel Ostracon." BJPES 13 (1947): 115–18 (Hebrew).

244. ———. "The 'Jerusalem' and 'The City' Stamps on Jar-handles." JPOS 13 (1933): 226–31.

245. Torczyner, H. "The Siloam Inscription, the Gezer Calendar and the Ophel Ostracon." BJPES 7 (1939): 4ff.

246. Vernes, M. "Note sur un fragment de vase antique, portant des caractères d'ancien phénicien, découvert à Jérusalem." CRAIBL, n.s. 6 (1870): 279–83.

247. Vincent, L. H. "Les Fouilles récentes d'Ophel." RB, n.s. 9 (1912): 549.

247a. ———. "Bulletin." RB 34 (1925): 476.

248. Vogue, C. J. M. *Inscriptions hébraiques de Jérusalem*. Paris, 1864; excerpt, Rev Arch A (1864–): 200–209.

249. Y. Yadin, ed., *Jerusalem Revealed. Archaeology in the Holy City 1968–1974*. New Haven, Conn., 1976.

Khirbet Beit Lei

250. Cross, F. M. "The Cave Inscriptions from Khirbet Beit Lei." In J. A. Sanders, ed., *Near Eastern Archaeology in the Twentieth Century*. New York, 1970. 299–306.

251. Lemaire, A. "Prières en temps de crise: les inscriptions de Khirbet Beit Lei." RB 83 (1976): 558–68.

252. Naveh. J. "Old Hebrew Inscriptions in a Burial Cave." IEJ 13 (1963): 74–92.

253. ———. "Old Hebrew Inscriptions in a Tomb Cave from the Period of the First Temple." BIES 27 (1963): 235–56 (Hebrew).

Khirbet el-Kom

254. Barag, D. "Note on an Inscription from Khirbet el-Qom." IEJ 20 (1970): 216–18.

255. Dever, W. G. "Inscriptions from Khirbet el-Kom." Qad 4 (1971): 90–92.

Ostracon No. 2 from Lachish. *(Courtesy of the Trustees of the Bristish Museum)*

256.   ———. "Iron Age Epigraphic Material from the Area of Khirbet el-Kom." HUCA 40–41 (1969–1970): 139–204.

257.   Geraty, L. T. "Third Century B.C. Ostraca from Khirbet el-Kom." HThR 65 (1972): 595–96.

257a.   ———. "Recent Suggestions on the Bilingual Ostracon from Khirbet el-Kom." AUSS 19 (1981): 137–40.

258.   Lemaire, A. "Les Inscriptions de Khirbet el-Qôm et l'ashérah de YHWH." RB 84 (1977): 595–608.

258a.   ———. "Une Nouvelle cruche inscrite en paléo-hebreu." *Maarav* 2 (1980): 159–62.

258b.   Mittman, S. "Die Grabinschrift des Sängers Uriahu." ZDPV 97 (1981): 139–52.

259.   Skaist, A. "A Note on the Bilingual Ostracon from Khirbet el-Kom." IEJ 28 (1978): 106–8.

LACHISH (TELL ED-DUWEIR)

260.   Aharoni, Y. "Trial Excavation in the 'Solar Shrine' at Lachish: Preliminary Report." IEJ 18 (1968): 157–69.

261.   Albright, W. F. "The Lachish Letters after Five Years." BASOR 82 (1941): 18–24.

262.   ———. "The Oldest Hebrew Letters; The Lachish Ostraca." BASOR 70 (1938): 11–17.

263.   ———. "A Re-examination of the Lachish Letters." BASOR 73 (1939): 16–21.

264.   ———. "Supplement to Jeremiah: The Lachish Ostraca." BASOR 61 (1936): 10–16.

265.   Balazs, G. *A Lachisi (Tell ed-Duweiri) asatasok archeologiai es epigrafiai eredmenyei.* Budapest, 1940.

266.   Birnbaum, S. "The Lachish Ostraca I." PEQ 71 (1939): 20–28, 91–110.

267.   Burrows, M. "I Have Written on the Door (Lachish Letter IV)." JAOS 56 (1936): 491–93.

268.   Burrows, E. "The Tell Duweir Ewer Inscription." PEFQS 66 (1934): 179–80.

269.   Cassuto, U. "Due nuovi sigilli ebraici scoperti a Lākīš." RSO 16 (1935–36): 160–62.

270.   Cross, F. M. "Lachish Letter IV." BASOR 144 (1956): 24–26.

270a.   Davies, G. I. "Tell Ed-Duweir = Ancient Lachish: A Response to G. W. Ahlström." PEQ 114 (1982): 25–28.

271.   Degen, R. "Der Räucheralter aus Lachish." NESE 1 (1972): 39–48.

271a.   Demsky, A. "A Note on 'Smoked Wine.'" TA 6 (1979): 163.

272.   Diringer, D. "Addendum to my Article on Ancient Hebrew Inscriptions Discovered at Tell ed-Duweir (Lachish)." PEQ 74 (1942): 103–4.

273.   ———. "On Ancient Hebrew Inscriptions Discovered at Tell ed-Duweir (Lachish), I–II." PEQ 73 (1941): 38–56, 89–109; "III." PEQ 75 (1943): 89–99.

274.   ———. "The Early Hebrew Weights Found at Lachish." PEQ 74 (1942): 82–103.

275.   ———. "Note on Some Jar-Stamps and Seals Discovered at Lachish." PEQ 75 (1943): 55–56.

275a.   Driver, G. R. "Old and New Semitic Texts." PEQ 70 (1938) 188–91.

276.   Dussaud, R. "Le Prophète Jérémie et les lettres de Lakish." *Syria* 19 (1938): 256–71.

277.   Elliger, K. "Lachish Ostraka." PJB 34 (1938): 30–58.

278.   ———. "Zu Text und Schrift der Ostraka von Lachis." ZDPV 62 (1939): 63–89.

279.   Ganor, N. R. "The Lachish Letters." PEQ 99 (1967): 74–77.

280.   Gaster, T. H. *The Archaic Inscriptions: Lachish II.* Oxford, 1940. 49–57.

281.   Ginsberg, H. L. "Concerning the Lachish Letters." BJPES 3 (1935): 77–86 (Hebrew).

Ostracon No. 3 (reverse) from Lachish. (*Courtesy of the Israel Department of Antiquities and Museums*)

Ostracon No. 3 (obverse) from Lachish. (*Courtesy of the Israel Department of Antiquities and Museums*)

282. ———. "Lachish Notes." BASOR 71 (1938): 24–27.

283. ———. "Lachish Ostraca New and Old." BASOR 80 (1940): 10–13.

284. Gordon, C. H. "Lachish Letter IV." BASOR 67 (1937): 30–32.

285. ———. "Notes on the Lachish Letters." BASOR 70 (1938): 17–18.

286. Hempel, J. "Die Ostraka von Lakis." ZAW, n.s. 15 (1938): 126–39.

287. Hanpert, R. S. "The Lachish Letters." BA 1 (1938): 30–32.

288. Hooke, S. H. "An Israelite Seal from Tell Duweir." PEFQS 66 (1934): 97–98.

289. ———. "Supplementary Note on the Tell Duweir Scarab." PEQ 68 (1936): 38; "Notes and News," PEQ 68 (1936): 118.

290. ———. "A Scarab and Sealing from Tell Duweir." PEQ 67 (1935): 195–97.

291. Inge, C. H. "Excavations at Tell ed-Duweir." PEQ 69 (1938): 240–56.

291a. ———. "Post-Scriptum (to Diringer, 'On Ancient Hebrew Inscriptions Discovered at Tell ed-Duweir, I–II' PEQ 73 (1941): 38–56, 89–109)." PEQ 73 (1941): 106–9.

292. Jack, J. W. "The Lachish Letters, Their Date and Import." PEQ 70 (1938): 165–87.

293. Jepsen, A. "Kleine Bemerkungen zu drei Westsemitischen Inschriften, 3. Lachish II, V and VI." MIO 15 (1969): 1–5.

294. *Lachish . . . (Tell ed Duweir) . . . .* London, New York, etc. Pub. for the Trustees of the late Sir Henry Wellcome by the Oxford University Press, 1938–1958. 4 vols. At head of title: The Wellcome Archaeological Research Expedition to the Near East (vol. 1); also, The Wellcome-Marston Archaeological Research Expedition to the Near East (vol. 2).

294a. Lemaire, A. "A Note on Inscription XXX from Lachish." TA 7 (1980): 92–4.

295. May, H. G. "Lachish Letter IV:7–10." BASOR 97 (1945): 22–25.

296. Michaud H. "Les Ostraca de Lakis conservés à Lourdes," Syria 35 (1957): 39–60.

297. Naveh, J. "A Hebrew Letter from the Time of Jeremiah." Arch 15 (1962): 108–11.

298. Neiman, D. *The Lachish Letters, 1950.* A.M. Thesis, University of Chicago, 1950.

299. Obermann, J. "The Archaic Inscriptions from Lachish." JAOS 58 (1938): supplement, 1–48.

300.   van den Oudenrign, M. A. *Les Fouilles de Lakis et l'étude de L'Ancien Testament*. Fribourg, 1942.

301.   Reider, J. "The Lachish Letters." JQR 29 (1939), 225–39.

302.   Sayce, A. H. "The Cuneiform and Other Inscriptions Found at Lachish and Elsewhere in the South of Palestine." PEFQS 25 (1938): 31.

303.   Simons, J. "Twee Nieuwgevonden Zegels uit het Bijbelsche Lachish." *Studien* 136 (1941): 14–16.

303a. Starkey, J. L. "Excavations at Tell ed-Duweir, 1934–1935." PEQ 67 (1935): 206.

304.   ———. "Excavations at Tell ed-Duweir, 1935–1936." PEQ 68 (1936): 178–89.

305.   ———. "Excavations at Tell ed-Duweir," PEQ 69 (1937):228–41.

Ostracon No. 5 from Lachish. *(Courtesy of the Trustees of the British Museum)*

306. ———. "Lachish as Illustrating Bible History," PEQ 69 (1937) 171–79.

307. Sukenik, E. L. "Note on a Jar Stamp Discovered at Tell ed-Duweir." PEQ 74 (1942): 57.

308. Thomas, D. "Again 'The Prophet' in the Lachish Ostraca." BZAW 77 (1958): 244–49.

309. ———. "The Age of Jeremiah in the Light of Recent Archaeological Discovery." PEQ 82 (1950): 1–5.

310. ———. "Jerusalem in the Lachish Ostraca." PEQ 78 (1946) 86–91.

311. ———. "Lachish Letters." JTS 40 (1939): 1–15.

312. ———. "The Lachish Ostraca." *Melilah* 3–4 (1950): 55–66.

313. ———. "The Lachish Ostraca; Professor Torczyner's Latest Views." PEQ 78 (1946): 38–42.

314. ———. "Ostracon III:13–18 from Tell ed-Duweir." PEQ 80 (1948): 131–36.

315. ———. "Ostraca XIX–XXI from Tell ed-Duweir (Lachish)." *Essays and Studies Presented to Stanley Arthur Cook*. London, 1950. 51–58.

316. ———. *The Prophet in the Lachish Ostraca*. London, 1946.

317. ———. "The Site of Ancient Lachish: The Evidence of Ostracon IV from Tell ed-Duweir." PEQ 72 (1940): 148ff.

318. Thompson, J. A. "On Some Stamps and a Seal from Lachish." BASOR 86 (1942): 24–27.

319. Torczyner, H. *The Lachish Ostraca; Letters from the Days of Jeremiah the Prophet*. Jerusalem, 1940 (Hebrew).

320. ———; Harding, G. L.; Lewis, A.; and Starkey, J. L. *Lachish I. The Lachish Letters*. Oxford, 1938.

321. Tufnell, O. *Lachish III. The Iron Age;* with contributions by A. Murray and D. Diringer. Oxford, 1953.

322. ———. *Lachish IV (Tell ed-Duweir); The Bronze Age*. London, 1958.

323. ———; Inge, C. H.; and Harding, G. L. *Lachish II: The Fosse Temple*. Oxford, 1940.

324. Ussishkin, D. "Answers at Lachish," BAR 5 (1979): 16–39.

325. ———. "The Destruction of Lachish by Sennacherib and the Dating of the Royal Judean Storage Jars." TA 4 (1977): 28–60.

326. ———. "Excavations at Tel Lachish, 1973–1977." TA 5 (1978): 1–97.

326a. ———. "*Lamelekh* Store-Jars and the Excavations at Lachish." Qad 9 (1976): 63–68.

327. ———. "Royal Judean Storage Jars and Private Seal Impressions." BASOR 223 (1976): 1–13.

The Seal and Impression of "Ahimelek (son of) Samek" from Lachish. (*Courtesy of the Israel Department of Antiquities and Museums*)

328. Vaccari, A. "Le Lettre de Lâchis," Bib 20 (1939): 180–99.

329. deVaux, R. "Les Ostraka de Lâchis." RB 48 (1939): 181–206.

330. Vincent, L. H. "Les Fouilles de Tell ed-Douweir = Lachis." RB 48 (1939): 406–30.

MEGIDDO (TELL EL-MUTESELIM)

331. Guthe, H.; Erman, A.; and Kautzsch, E. "Ein Siegelstein mit Hebräischer Unterschrift vom Tell el-Mutesellim." MNDPV 5 (1906): 33–5.

332. Guy, P. L. O. and Engberg, R. M. *Megiddo Tombs*. Chicago, 1938.

333. Lamon, R. S., and Shipton, G. M. *Megiddo I. Seasons of 1925–1934. Strata I–V*. Chicago, 1939.

334. May, H. G. "An Inscribed Jar from Megiddo." AJSL 50 (1933–1934): 10–14.

335. Schumacher, G., and Steuernagel, C. *Tell el-Mutesellim I*. Leipzig, 1908. 99–100.

336. Staples, W. E. "An Inscribed Scaraboid from Megiddo." In P. L. O. Guy, ed., *New Light from Armageddon. Second Provisional Report (1927–1929) on the Excavations at Megiddo in Palestine*. Chicago, Oriental Institute Communications 9, 1931. 49–68, figs. 33–34.

337. Watzinger, C. *Tell el-Mutesellim II*. Leipzig, 1929.

338. Yeivin, S. "The Hamman Scaraboid from Megiddo." BJPES 9 (1942): 78–79.

RAMAT RAHEL (BETH HACCHEREM)

339. Aharoni, Y. "Excavations at Ramat Rahel, 1954." IEJ 6 (1956): 137–57.

340. ———. *Excavations at Ramat Rahel, Seasons 1959–1960*. Vol. 1. Rome, 1962; *Seasons 1961–1962*. Vol. 2. Rome, 1964.

341. ———. "Excavations at Ramat Rahel." BA 24 (1961): 98–118.

342. ———. "Five Seasons of Excavation at Ramat Rahel." BIES 24 (1959): 73–119 (Hebrew).

343. ———. "Hebrew Jar Stamps from Ramat Rahel." EI 6 (1960): 56–60 (Hebrew).

SAMARIA (SEBASTIYEH)

344. Able, F. M. "Un Mot sur les ostraca de Samarie." RB 8 (1911): 290–92.

345. Aharoni, Y. "The Samaria Ostraca: an Additional Note." IEJ 12 (1962): 67–69.

346. Albright, W. F. "Ostracon C 1101 of Samaria." PEQ 68 (1936): 211–15.

347. ———. "Researches of the School in West Judea." BASOR 15 (1924): 2–11.

348. ———. "The Site of Tirzah and the Topography of Western Manasseh." JPOS 11 (1931): 241–51.

349. Alt, A. "Das Institut im Jahr 1931, 5. Die Reise." PJB 28 (1932): 18ff.

350. Ben-Dor, I., "A Hebrew Seal from Samaria." QDAP 12 (1946): 78–83.

351. Chaplin, T. "An Ancient Hebrew Weight from Samaria." PEFQS 22 (1890): 265–68.

352. Conder, C. R. "The Hebrew Weight." PEFQS 23 (1891): 69ff.

353. ———. "The Hematite Weight." PEFQS 27 (1895): 191.

354. Cook, S. A. "Reviews and Notices of Publications." PEFQS 44 (1912): 48.

355. ———. "Reviews and Notices of Publications." PEFQS 48 (1916): 151–53.

356. ———. "Reviews and Notices of Publications." PEFQS 58 (1926): 47–48.

357. Cross, F. M. "Epigraphic Notes on Hebrew Documents of the Eighth–Sixth Centuries B.C., I. A New Reading of a Place Name in the Samaria Ostraca." BASOR 163 (1961): 12–14.

358. Crowfoot, J. W.; Kenyon, K. M.; and Sukenik, E. L. Samaria-Sebaste 1: The Buildings at Samaria. London, 1942.

359. Crowfoot, J. W. and G. M. Samaria-Sebaste 2: Early Ivories from Samaria. London, 1938.

360. Crowfoot, J. W. and G. M. and Kenyon, K. M. Samaria-Sebaste 3: The Objects from Samaria. London, 1957.

361. Davis, E. "Note on the Hematite Weight from Samaria." PEFQS 27 (1895): 187–90.

362. Decroix, J. "Les Ostraca de Samarie." BiTerS 120 (1970): 15–17.

363. Dhorme, P. "L'Ancien Hébreu dans la vie courante." RB 39 (1930): 63ff.

364. Diringer, D. "The Dating of Early Hebrew Inscriptions, the Samaria Ostraca." PEQ 75 (1943): 50–54.

365. Dougherby, R. P. "Cuneiform Parallels to Solomon's Provisioning System." AASOR (1923–1924), 23–63.

366. Driver, R. "The Discoveries at Samaria." PEFQS 43 (1911): 79–83.

367. ———. "The Haematite Weight with an Inscription in Ancient Semitic Characters, Purchased at Samaria in 1890 by Thomas Chaplin, Esq. M.D." *The Academy*, 28 October 1893; PEFQS 26 (1894): 220–25.

368. Dussaud, R. "Samarie au temps d'Achab." Syria 6 (1925): 314–38, Syria 7 (1926): 9–29.

369. Galling, K. "Eine Ostrakon aus Samaria als Rechtsurkund." ZDPV 77 (1961): 173–85.

370. Gray, G. B. "A Group of Hebrew Names of the Ninth Century B.C." Expos. Times 27 (1915): 57–62.

371. Gressmann, H. "Die Ausgrabungen in Samaria." ZAW 43 (1925): 147–50.

372. Hoelscher, G. "Die Neuen Funde von Samaria." MNDPV 17 (1911): 22–28.

373. Israel, F. "L' 'olio da toeletta' negli ostraca di Samaria." RSO 49/1–2 (1975): 17–20.

374. Jack, J. W. *Samaria in Ahab's Time, Harvard Excavations and their Results with Chapters on the Political and Religious Situation.* Edinburgh, 1929.

375. Jirku, A. "Das Inschriftenmaterial der Amerikanischen Ausgrabungen in Samaria." OLZ 28 (1925): col. 273–80.

376. Kaufman, I. T. "A Note on the Place Name *SPR* and the Letter Samek in the Samaria Ostraca." BASOR 172 (1963): 60–61.

377. ———. The Samaria Ostraca: A Study in Ancient Hebrew Paleography." HThR 60 (1967): 491–92.

377a. Kaufman, I. T. "The Samaria Ostraca: An Early Witness to Hebrew Writing." BA 45 (1982): 229–39.

378. Kittel, R. "Merkwürdige Funde im Alten Samaria." *Theologisches Literaturblatt* 32 (1911): 3ff., 49–54, 73–76.

379. Koenig, E. "Die Neuesten Schriftfunde in Palästina." *Zeitschrift für des Evangelischen Religionsunterr* 20 (1911): 305–13.

380. Lemaire, A. "L'Ostracon 1101 de Samarie. Nouvel essai." RB 79 (1972): 565–70.

381. Lindblom, J. "Der Buchstabe *zeta* im Phönizisch-Griechischen Alphabet." In *E Symbolae Philologicis O. A. Danielsson Octogenario Dicatis Seorsum Expressum.* Upsala, 1932. 153f.

382. Lyon, D. G. "Hebrew Ostraca from Samaria." HThR 4 (1911): 136–43, 267.

382a. Macridy-Bey, "Erwerbungen des Kaiserlich-Ottomanliches Museums in Konstantinopel im Jahre 1911." AA (1911), 583–88.

383. Maisler, B. "Der Destrikt *Śrq* in den Samaritanischen Ostraka." JPOS 14 (1934): 96–100.

384. ———. "The Historical Background of the Samaria Ostraca." JPOS 22 (1948): 117–33.

385. Masterman, E. W. G. "Communication." PEFQS 43 (1911): 2.

386. ———. "The Harvard Excavations at Samaria, 4: The Ostraka." PEFQS 57 (1925): 30.

387. Moore, G. F. "Hebrew Ostraca of the Ninth Century from Samaria." AJA 15 (1911): 70.

388. Nestle, E. "Redende Scherben." *Evangelischen Kirchenblatt für Würtemberg* 72 (1911): 143.

389. "Notes and News." PEFQS 51 (1919): 149.

390. Noth, M. "Der Beitrag der Samarischen Ostraca zur Lösung Topographischer Fragen." PJB 28 (1932): 54–68.

391. ———. "Exkursus über die Zahlzeichen auf den Ostraka." ZDPV 50 (1927): 240ff.

392. ———. "Das Krongut der Israelitischen Könige und Seine Verwaltung, 2. Die Samarischen Ostraka." ZDPV 50 (1927): 219–44.

393. O'Doherty, E. "The Date of the Ostraca of Samaria." CBQ 15 (1953): 24–29.

394. Parrot, A. *Samaria: The Capital of the Kingdom of Israel.* London, 1958.

395. Rainey, A. F. "Administration in Ugarit and the Samaria Ostraca." IEJ 12 (1962): 62–63.

396. ———. "The Samaria Ostraca in the Light of Fresh Evidence." PEQ 99 (1967): 32–41.

397. ———. "Semantic Parallels to the Samaria Ostraca." PEQ 102 (1970): 45–51

397a. ———. "The *Sitz im Leben* of the Samaria Ostraca." TA 6 (1979): 91–94.

398. Reisner, G. *Israelite Ostraca from Samaria.* Boston, 192?.

399. ———; Fischer, C. S.; and Lyon, D. G. *Harvard Excavations at Samaria, 1908–1910, I Text. II Plates.* Cambridge, 1924.

399a. Sasson, V. "*smn rḥṣ* in the Samaria Ostraca." JSS 26 (1981): 1–5.

400. Sayce, A. H. "Ahab's Palace at Samaria." Expos. Times 22 (1911): 527ff.

401. ———. "The Inscribed Weight from Samaria." *The Academy,* 23 December 1893; PEFQS 26 (1894): 285–86.

402. ———, and Chaplin, T. "The Ancient Hematite Weight from Samaria." PEFQS 26 (1894): 284ff.

403. Shea, W. H. "The Date and Significance of the Samaria Ostraca." IEJ 27 (1977): 16–27.

404.   Sukenik, E. L. "Inscribed Hebrew and Aramaic Potsherds from Samaria." PEFQS 65 (1933): 152–54.

406.   ———. "Inscribed Potsherds with Biblical Names from Samaria." PEFQS 65 (1933): 200ff.

407.   ———. "An Israelite Gem from Samaria." PEFQS 60 (1928):51ff.

408.   ———. "Note on a Fragment of an Israelite Stele Found at Samaria." PEFQS 68 (1936): 156.

409.   ———. "Notes on Hebrew Letters on the Ivories," In J. W. and G. M. Crowfoot, eds., *Samaria-Sebaste 2* (London, 1938): 6–8.

410.   ———. "Potsherds from Samaria Inscribed with the Divine Name." PEFQS 68 (1936): 34–37.

411.   Tyler, T. "The Methods of Higher Criticism." *The Academy*, 25 November 1893; PEFQS 26 (1894): 285.

412.   Vincent, L. H. "Communication 26," RB 8 (1911): 131; OLZ 15 (1911): 91, 235 (correction).

413.   ———. "Review of Reisner's *Harvard Excavations at Samaria 1908–1910*." RB 34 (1925): 436–41.

414.   Yadin, Y. "Ancient Judean Weights and the Date of the Samaria Ostraca." In C. Rabin, ed., *Scripta Hierosolymitana Vol. III, Studies in the Bible.* Jerusalem, 1961.

415.   ———. "A Further Note on the *Lamed* in the Samaria Ostraca." IEJ 18 (1968): 50–51.

416.   ———. "A Further Note on the Samaria Ostraca." IEJ 12 (1962): 64–66.

417.   ———. "Recipients or Owners: A Note on the Samaria Ostraca." IEJ 9 (1959): 184–87.

418.   ———. "Tax-Payers or Tax-Collectors (On the Problem of the *l^e* in the Samaria Ostraca)." BIES 24 (1959): 17–21.

SHECHEM (TELL BALATA)

419.   Bohl, F. M. Th. "Die Sichem Plakette." ZDPV 61 (1938): 1–25.

420.   Cross, F. M. "An Inscribed Seal from Balatah (Shechem)." BASOR 167 (1962): 14–15.

421.   Kerkhof, V. J. "An Inscribed Stone Weight from Shechem." BASOR 184 (1966): 20–21.

422.   Wright, G. E. "Selected Seals from the Excavations at Balatah (Shechem)." BASOR 167 (1962): 5–13.

423.   Wright, G. E. *Shechem: The Biography of a Biblical City.* New York, 1965.

The Siloam Tunnel Inscription. *(Courtesy of the Istanbul Arkeoloji Müzeleri Müdürlüğü)*

SHIQMONA

424. Cross, F. M. "Jar Inscriptions from Shiqmona." IEJ 18 (1968): 226–33.
425. Elgavish, J. *Shiqmona*. Haifa, 1968– .
425a. Van den Branden, A. "Le Disque de bronze de Shiqmona." BeO 22 (1980): 219–225.

SILOAM

426. Amiran, R. "The Water Supply of Israelite Jerusalem." In Y. Yadin, ed., *Jerusalem Revealed*. New Haven, Conn., 1976. 75–78.
427. ———. "The Water Supply of Jerusalem." Qad 1 (1967): 13–18 (Hebrew).
428. "The Ancient Hebrew Inscription in the Pool of Siloam." PEFQS 13 (1881): 282–85 (A. H. Sayce); 285–92 (C. R. Conder); 292–93 (I. Taylor); 293–96 (S. Beswick); 296ff. (H. Sulley).
428a. Anonymous. REJ 2 (1881): 314; 3 (1881): 147, 296, 305.
429. *The Athenaeum* 2 (1881): 80, 144 (M. W. Schapira); 112, 176, 239 (A. Neubauer); 208 (A. H. Sayce); 400 (I. Taylor); 496 (W. Besant).
430. Baedeker, C. *Palästina und Syrien*. Leipzig, 1900. 99.

431. Barrois, A. "Le Métrologie dans la Bible," RB 40 (1931): 195ff.

432. Berger, Ph. "L'Inscription de Siloé à Jérusalem." *Journal des Débats* 16 (April, 1882).

433. ————. "Les Inscriptions sémitiques et l'histoire." *Bulletin Hebdomadaire de L'Association Scientifique* 155, relazione fatta il 27 Fabbeaio, 1883.

434. Bertholet, A. "Der Älteste Tunnel." *Beilage zur Allgemeine Zeitung* 1 (1905): 431.

435. Beswick, S. " 'Siloam Tunnel,' with Annex of C. R. Conder." PEFQS 14 (1882): 178–83.

436. Birch, W. F. "The Siloam Inscription." PEFQS 22 (1890): 208–10.

437. ————. "The Valley of Hinnom." PEFQS 41 (1909): 299ff.

438. Blake, F. R. "Notes on the Siloam Inscription." *Johns Hopkins University Circulars* 22/163 (1903): 62ff.

439. ————. "The Word *zdh* in the Siloam Inscription." JAOS 22 (1901): 55–60.

440. Blau, L. "Wie Lange Stand die Althebräische Schrift bei den Judem im Gebrauch?" In *Gedenkbuch zur Erinnerung an David Kaufman*. Breslau, 1900. 56.

441. Bruston, Ch. "Additions aux inscriptions en Hébreu archaique." *Revue de Theologie et des Questions Religieuses* 20 (1911): 175ff.

442. ————. *L'Inscription de Siloé et celle d'Eschmounazar*. Paris, 1904.

443. ————. *Les Inscriptions en Hébreu archaique et celle d'Eschmounazar*. Paris, 1909.

444. ————. "*zdh* dans l'inscription de Siloé." ZAW 29 (1909): 155.

445. Carus, P. "The Siloam Inscription." *The Open Court* 17 (1901): 662–67.

446. Caspari, W. "Die Siloahinschrift, Ein Werk der Nachexilischen Renaissance." *Neue Kirchliche Zeitung* 22 (1911): 873–905, 907–34.

447. Chajes, H. P. "Iscrizioni nell'ebraismo antico." *Rivista Israelitica* 2/2 (1905).

448. Clermont-Ganneau, Ch. "Forged Inscription in Hebrew Phoenician." PEFQS 6 (1874): 90ff.

449. ————. *Les Fraudes archéologiques en Palestine I. Inscriptions authentiques de Palestine antérieures à la prise Jérusalem par Titus*. Bibliothèque Orientale Elzévirienne, vol. 40, 1885.

450. ————. "Genuine and False Inscriptions in Palestine." PEFQS 16 (1884): 75.

451. ————. "L'Inscription hébraique de l'aqueduc de Siloé." RAO 1 (1888): 293–99.

452. ————. "L'Inscription israélite de l'aqueduc de Siloé." RAO 6 (1905): 107–11.

453.   ———. "Mission en Palestine et en Phénicie, Ve Rapport." *Archives des Missions Scientifiques et Litteraires*, Series 3, vol. 11, p. 203.

454.   ———. "Notes." PEFQS 14 (1882): 17ff.

455.   ———. "Sur les dimensions des cartouches contenant les inscriptions hébraiques archaiques." RAO 1 (1888): 399ff.

456.   ———. "Les Tombeaux de David et des rois de Juda et le tunnel-aqueduc de Siloé." CRAIBL 4, 25 (1897): 383–427; RAO 2 (1897): 254–94.

457.   ———. "Topographie de la Jérusalem antique," RAO 8 (1907): 27.

458.   ———. RA 36 (1900): 157 (Siloam Inscription).

459.   ———. "Note sull'iscrizione del *Šiloah:* lettera al Renan," Revue Archéologique n.s. 42 (1881): 251.

460.   Cohen, N. "*zdh* in the Siloam Inscription." *Beth Miqra* 15 (1970): 359–60 (Hebrew).

461.   Conder, C. R. "Date of the Siloam Text." PEFQS 29 (1897): 204–8.

462.   ———. "Notes," PEFQS 26 (1894): 301ff.

463.   ———. "The Siloam Tunnel." PEFQS 14 (1882): 122–31.

464.   Dahse, J. "Die Lage der Quellen von II Cr. 32:30, 33:14 nach der LXX." ZAW 28 (1908): 1–5.

465.   Daniel, M. "L'Inscription hébraïque de la Piscine de Siloé." *L'Univers* 7 (1885).

466.   Davis, E. "The Siloam and Later Palestinian Inscriptions Considered in Relation to Sacred Textual Criticism." PEFQS 26 (1894): 269–77.

467.   Derenbourg, J. "L'Inscription du tunnel près de la fontaine de Šiloé, à Jérusalem." CRAIBL, ser. 4, 9 (1881): 97–100, 199–205.

468.   ———. "L'Inscription hébraïque du Šiloah près de Jérusalem." REJ 3 (1881): 161–72.

469.   Ducati, B. "La scrittura." *Bollettino dell'Accademia Italiana di Stenografia* 7 (April 1931): 9.

470.   Duncan, J. G. *Digging up Biblical History, II.* n.p., 1931.

471.   Ebers, G., and Guthe, H. *Palästina in Wort und Bild.* Stuttgart, 1883. 1: 492.

472.   Feilchenfeld, W. "Die Siloahinscrift in Jerusalem." *Magazin für Judische Geschichte and Literatur* 9 (1883): 145–51.

473.   Finegan, J. *Light from the Ancient Past.* Princeton, N.J., 1946.

474.   Fischer, A. "Zur Siloahinscrift." ZDMG 56 (1902): 800–809.

475.   Frohnmeyer, I., and Benzinger, I. *Vues et Documents Bibliques.* Paris, 1905. 94, 145f.

476. Garbini, G. "L'iscrizione di Siloe e gli 'Annali dei re di Guida.'" AIUON 19 (1969): 261–63.

477. Gorg, M. "Ein problematisches Wort der Siloah-Inscrift." BN 11 (1980): 21–22.

478. Gossler, P. "An den Wassern von Siloah." *Stimmen des Orients* 1 (1923): 194–99.

479. Guthe, H. "Ausgrabungen bei Jerusalem." ZDPV 5 (1882): 85ff.

480. ———. "Die Echte und die Gefälschte Siloahinschrift." ZDPV 13 (1890): 203ff.

481. ———. "Das Schicksal der Siloah-Inschrift." ZDPV 13 (1890): 286–88.

482. ———. "Die Siloahinschrift." ZDMG 36 (1882): 725–50.

483. ———. "Ueber die Siloahinschrift." *The Athenaeum* 2 (1881): 116–18, 250–59.

484. Halevy, J. "Mélanges, XI: *zdh* (Inscription de Siloé)." *Mélanges de Critique et d'Histoire* 20 (1883): 431.

485. ———. *Revue Critique* 42 (1881): 292; JA 17 (1881): 552 (Siloam Inscription).

485a. Hoelscher, G. ZDPV 33 (1910): 55f (Siloam Inscription).

486. Hommel, F. *Geschichte des Alten Morgenländes.* Leipzig, 1908. 149f.

487. "Le iscrizioni della Palestine." *La Civiltà Cattolica*, ser. 12, 12 (1885): 25ff.

488. Jepsen, A. "Kleine Bemerkungen zu drei Westsemitischen Inschriften 2. Zu Text und Aufbau der Siloah-Inschrift, 2–4." MIO 15 (1969): 1–5.

489. Kautzsch, E. "Die Hebräische Inschrift im Siloah-Canal." *Beilage zur Augsburger Allgemeine Zeitung* 119 (1881): 1739ff.

490. ———. "Nachträgliches zur Siloahinschrift." ZDPV 5 (1882): 205–18.

491. ———. "Die Siloahinschrift." ZDPV 4 (1881): 102–14, 260–71.

492. Kuemmel, A. *Materialien zur Topographie des alten Jerusalem.* Halle, 1906. 174f.

493. Lambert, M. REJ 79 (1924): 214ff. (Siloam Inscription).

494. Levi Della Vida, G. "The Shiloah Inscription Reconsidered." In M. Black and G. Fohrer, eds., *Memoriam P. Kahle.* Berlin, 1968. 162–66.

495. Lidzbarski, M. "Review of Albert Socin, *Die Siloahinschrift zum Gebrauch bei Akademischen Vorlesungen.*" DLZ 21 (1900): 734ff.

496. Livini, I. "The Siloam Inscription." BJPES 9 (1942): 114ff. (Hebrew).

497. Luncz, A. M. "Die Entdeckung Einer Alten Inschrift." *Jerusalem* 1 (1881–1882): 168–74.

498. ———. "The Siloah or the Gihon." *Luaḥ Erets Yisrael* 7 (1901): 157–62.

499. Marti, K. "Miscellen. 8. Zur Siloahinschrift." ZAW 28 (1908): 152.

500. Merril, S. "The Siloam Inscription." *The American Antiquarian and Biblical Journal* 4 (1881): 71ff.

501. Michaud, H. "Un Passage difficile dans l'inscription de Siloé." VT 8 (1958): 297–302.

502. ———. "Réserrement ou animation?" VT 9 (1959): 205–9.

503. Mommert, C. *Siloah. Brunnen, Teich, Kanal zu Jerusalem*. Leipzig, 1908.

504. Montgomery, J. A. "The Holy City and Gehenna." JBL 27 (1908): 24–47.

505. Neubauer, A. REJ I (1881): 333–35.

506. Opinioni del Gildemeister, del Nöldeke e del Budde; letteri di A. Hochmuth (Guthe, 1881): W. Feilchenfeld (Kautzsch, 1881); A. Beck (Socin, 1881); K. Marti (1882), F. Delitzsch (1882)." ZDPV 5 (1882): 205ff.

507. Peiser, F. E. "Aus dem Kaiserlich Ottomanischen Museum in Constantinopel." OLZ 1 (1898): cols. 6–9.

508. Pilcher, E. J. "The Date of the Siloam Inscription," PSBA 19 (1897): 165–82.

509. ———. "Herodian Pottery and the Siloam Inscription." PSBA 20 (1898): 213–22.

510. ———, and Davis, E. "On the Date of the Siloam Inscription." PEFQS 30 (1898): 55–60.

511. Praetorius, F. "Zur Siloahinschrift." ZDMG 60 (1906): 403.

512. Press, J. *Palästina und Südsyrien*. Jerusalem, 1921. 165.

513. ———. *Erets Israel and the Region of Syria*. Jerusalem, 1921. 186 (Hebrew).

514. "Protokollarischer Bericht über die in Berlin am 14, September 1881 Abgehaltene Zweite Generalversammlung des Deutschen Vereins zur Erforschung Palästinas." Edited by E. Kautzsch and J. Halevy. ZDPV 5 (1882): 8.

515. Puech, E. "L'Inscription du tunnel de Siloé." RB 81 (1974): 196–214.

516. Punier. *Theologischer Jahresbericht* 2 (1883): 10; 3 (1884): 9 (Siloam Inscription).

517. Renan, E. "Rapport annuel sur les travaux du Conseil de la Société Asiatique (30/1882)." JA 7, 20 (1882): 44–45.

518. Rothstein, G. "Siloam Inscription." *Berliner Philologische Wochenschrift* 29 (1909): 1056–58.

518a. Sasson, V. "The Siloam Tunnel Inscription." PEQ 114 (1982): 111–17.

519. Sayce, A. H. *The Ancient Hebrew Inscription Discovered at the Pool of Siloam in Jerusalem*. London, 1881.

520. ———. "The Ancient Hebrew Inscription Discovered at the Pool of Siloam in Jerusalem." PEFQS 13 (1881): 141–53. "II. Postscriptum." Ibid., 153–54. "III. The Date of the Siloam Inscription" (I. Taylor). Ibid., 155–57.

521. ———. "The Ancient Hebrew Inscription of Siloam." *Records of the Past*, n.s. 1 (1888): 168–75.

522. ———. "The Inscription of the Pool of Siloam," PEFQS 13 (1881): 69–73.

523. ———. "The Oldest Jewish Inscription." *The Athenaeum* 1 (1881): 364–94 (with remarks of A. Neubauer, p. 395).

524. ———. "The Siloam Inscription." PEFQS 14 (1882): 62ff.

525. Schaefer, J. *Der Katholik* 40 (1909): 72ff (Siloam Inscription).

526. Schencke, W. *Hvad Jorden Giemte. Om Utgrovninger og Textfund i Palestina og Nabslandene, Siloach Indskriften*. Christiania, 1911.

527. Schick, C. "Bericht über Meine Arbeiten am Siloahkanal." ZDPV 5 (1882): 1–6.

528. ———. "Phoenician Inscription in the Pool of Siloam." PEFQS 12 (1880): 180ff., 238.

529. Schwalleg, E. ThLZ 25 (1900): 163 (Siloam Inscription).

530. Sheppard, H. W. "Siloam." JTS 16 (1915): 414–16.

531. Sidersky, D. "L'Inscription de Siloé." JA 11, 11–12 (1918): 558–61.

532. ———. "L'Inscription hébraique de Siloé." Revue Archéologique 5/19 (1924): 117–31.

533. Smith, G. A. *Jerusalem, I–II*. London, 1907–1908. 1: 94f.

534. Socin, A. "Eine Neue Entdeckung in Jerusalem." ZDPV 3 (1880): 54ff.

535. ———. *Die Siloahinschrift zum Gebrauch bei Akademischen Vorlesungen*. Freiburg, 1899; ZDPV 22 (1899): 61–64.

536. Stoebe, H. J. "Überlegungen zur Siloahinschrift." ZDPV 71 (1955): 124–40.

537. ———. "Zu Vet. Test. VIII/5. 297ff." (Henri Michaud, "Un Passage difficile dans l'inscription Siloé.") VT 9 (1959): 99–101.

538. Taylor, I. *The Alphabet*. London, 1883. 1: 232–36.

538a. ———. "The Date of the Siloam Inscription." PEFQS 13 (1881): 155–57.

Tomb Inscriptions from Siloam Village. Top: "The tomb chamber in the side of the rock. . . ." Bottom: "This is (the tomb of . . .) yahu, who was over the house. . . ." *(Courtesy of the Trustees of the British Museum)*

539. Torczyner, H. "The Siloam Inscription, the Gezer Calendar and the Ophel Ostracon." BJPES 7 (1939): 4ff.

540. Torrey, C. C. "New Notes on Some Old Inscriptions; Siloam." ZA 26 (1911): 77–92.

541. Vincent, L. H. *Jérusalem sous terre. Les Récentes Fouilles d'Ophel.* London, 1911.

542. ———. "Note à propos du mémoire de M. Stanley A. Cook." RB, n.s. 7 (1901): 158–59.

543. Wordsworth, W. A. "The Siloam Inscription." PEQ 71 (1939): 41–43.

544. Wright, W. "Remarks on the Siloam Inscription." PSBA 4 (1881): 68–70.

SILOAM VILLAGE

545. N. Avigad, "The Epitaph of a Royal Steward from Siloam Village." IEJ 3 (1953): 137–52.

546. ———. "The Grave Inscription *yhw 'sr 'l hbyt.*" EI 3 (1954): 66–72 (Hebrew).

547. ———. "The Second Tomb-Inscription of the Royal Steward." IEJ 5 (1955): 163–66.

548.   Clermont-Ganneau, C. "Notes on Certain New Discoveries at Jerusalem, 1). Hebrew Inscription in Phoenician Characters." PEFQS 3 (1871): 103.

548a. Good, R. M. "The Israelite Royal Steward in the Light of Ugaritic *'l bt*." RB 86 (1979): 580–82.

549.   Katzenstein, H. J. "The Royal Steward." IEJ 10 (1960): 149–54.

550.   Reifenberg, A. "A Newly Discovered Hebrew Inscription of the Pre-Exilic Period." JPOS 21 (1948): 134–37.

551.   Ussishkin, D. "On the Short Inscription from the Tomb of '. . . yahu Who is over the House.'" *Leshonenu* 33 (1968–69): 297–303.

552.   ———. "On the Shorter Inscription from the 'Tomb of the Royal Steward.'" BASOR 196 (1969): 16–22.

553.   ———. "A Recently Discovered Monolithic Tomb in Siloam." In Y. Yadin, ed., *Jerusalem Revealed*. New Haven, Conn., 1976. 63–65.

554.   Wright, G. E. "Epitaph of a Judean Official." BA 17 (1954): 22–32.

TELL BEIT MIRSIM (DEBIR)

555.   Albright, W. F. "The American Excavations at Tell Beit Mirsim." ZAW 47 (1929): 1–17.

556.   ———. *The Excavation of Tell Beit Mirsim*. 4 vols. New Haven, Conn., 1932–1943.

557.   ———. "The Second Campaign at Tell Beit Misim (Kirjat-Sepher)." BASOR 31 (1928): 10–11.

558.   ———. "The Second Campaign at Tell Beit Mirsim." AFO 5 (1929): 119.

559.   ———. "The Third Campaign of Excavation at Tell Beit Mirsim." BASOR 38 (1930): 10; AFO 7 (1931): 58.

560.   Kyle, M. G. "Excavations at Tell Beit Mirsim, the Ancient Kirjath Sepher." BSa 85 (1928): 381–408.

TELL EL-FUL (GIBEAH)

561.   Albright, W. F. "Tell el-Ful." AASOR 4 (1922–23): 19–24.

TELL EL-HESI (EGLON)

562.   Albright, W. F. "A Neglected Hebrew Inscription from the Thirteenth Century B.C." AFO 5 (1929): 150–52.

562a. Bliss, F. J. *A Mound of Many Cities*. London, 1898.

563.   Clermont-Ganneau, C. "The Hebrew-Phoenician Inscription of Tell el-Hesy." PEFQS 24 (1892): 126–28.

564.   Conder, C. R. "The Tell el-Hesi Text." PEFQS 24 (1892): 203.

565.   Obermann, J. "A Revised Reading of the Tell el-Hesi Inscription with a Note on the Gezer Sherd." AJA 44 (1940): 93–104.

TELL EL-KHELEIFEH (EZION-GEBER, ELATH)

566.   Albright, W. F. "Ostracon no. 6043 from Ezion-geber." BASOR 82 (1941): 11–15.

567.   Glueck, N. "Ezion-geber." BA 28 (1965): 71–87.

568.   ———. "Ezion-geber: Elath—City of Bricks with Straw." BA 3 (1940): 51–55.

569.   ———. "Ezion-geber: Elath, the Gateway to Arabia." BA 2 (1939): 37–41, 43.

570.   ———. "The First Campaign at Tell el-Kheleifeh." BASOR 71 (1938): 3–17.

571.   ———. "Ostraca from Elath." BASOR 80 (1940): 3–9; BASOR 82 (1941): 3–11.

572.   ———. "Some Ezion-Geber: Elath Iron II Pottery." EI 9 (1969): 51–59.

573.   ———. "Tell el-Kheleifeh Inscriptions." In H. Goedicke, ed., *Near Eastern Studies in Honor of William Foxwell Ablright*. Baltimore, 1971. 225–42.

574.   ———. "The Third Season of Excavations at Tell el-Kheleifeh." BASOR 79 (1940): 2–17.

575.   ———. "The Topography and History of Ezion-Geber and Elath." BASOR 72 (1938): 2–12.

576.   Naveh, J. "The Scripts of Two Ostraca from Elath." BASOR 183 (1966) 27–30; BIES 30 (1966): 39–44.

577.   Rosenthal, F. "The Script of Ostracon 6043 from Ezion-Geber." BASOR 85 (1942): 8–9.

578.   Sukenik, E. L. "A Hebrew Seal from Ezion-Geber." *Kedem* 1 (1942): 95.

579.   Torrey, C. C. "On the Ostraca from Elath (Bulletin no. 80)." BASOR 82 (1941): 15–16.

TELL EN-NASBEH (MIZPAH)

580.   Bade, W. F. "The Excavations at Tell en-Nasbeh." PEFQS 59 (1927): 7–13.

581. ———. "A Jar Handle Stamp from Tell en-Nasbeh." ZAW 50 (1932): 89.

582. ———. "The Seal of Jaazaniah." ZAW 51 (1933): 150–56.

583. ———. *Some Tombs of Tell en-Nasbeh Discovered in 1929, a Special Report*. Berkeley, Palestine Institute Publications, nos. 1 and 2, 1928 and 1931.

584. ———. "The Tell en-Nasbeh Excavations of 1929. A Preliminary Report." PEFQS 62 (1930): 8–19.

585. Mastermann, E. W. G. "Miscellaneous Notes." PEFQS 61 (1929): 61–62

586. McCown, C. C. *Tell en-Nasbeh, I, Archaeological and Historical Results*. Berkeley-New Haven, 1947.

TELL ES-SAREM

587. Kallner, R. B. "Two Inscribed Sherds from Tell es-Sarem." *Kedem* 2 (1945): 11ff. (Hebrew).

588. Sukenik, E. L. "Note on the Sherd from Tell es-Sarem." *Kedem* 2 (1945): 15 (Hebrew).

TELL QASILE

589. Maisler, B. "Excavations at Tell Qasile." BJPES 15/1–2 (1949): 8–18.

590. ———. "The Excavations at Tell Qasile: Preliminary Report." IEJ 1 (1950–1951): 194–218.

591. ———. "Two Hebrew Ostraca from Tell Qasile." JNES 10 (1951): 265–67.

TELL ZAKARIYA (AZEKAH)

592. Bliss, F. J. "Fourth Report on the Excavations at Tell Zakariya." PEFQS 32 (1900): 7–16.

593. ———. "Second Report on the Excavations at Tell Zakariya." PEFQS 31 (1899): 89–111.

594. ———. "Reports on the Excavations at Tell Zakariya; Tell es-Safi; Tell el-Judeideh; Tell Sandahannah." PEFQS 31 (1899): 10ff., 89ff., 170ff., 198, 315ff.; PEFQS 32 (1900): 12ff., 94f., 207ff., 330ff.

595. Conder, C. R. "Tell Zakariya." PEFQS 31 (1899): 269–70.

596. Macalister, R. A. S. "The Rockcuttings of Tell Zakariya." PEFQS 31 (1899): 45ff.

597. Sayce, A. H. "Note on the Objects Discovered by Dr. Bliss at Tell-Zakariya." PEFQS 31 (1899): 210ff.

598. Vincent, L. H. "Les Fouilles anglaises à Tell Zakarîya." RB 8 (1899): 448ff. and 606ff.

Yavneh-Yam (Meṣad Ḥashavyahu)

599. Amusin, J. D., and Heltzer, M. L. "The Inscription from Meṣad Ḥashayahu. Complaints of a Reaper of the Seventh Century B.C." IEJ 14 (1964): 148–57.

600. Blaiklock, E. M. "The Man Who Lost His Cloak." *Eternity* 15 (1964): 27.

601. Brand, J. "Remarks on the Ḥashavyahu Letter." BIES 27 (1963): 206.

602. Cross, F. M. "Epigraphic Notes on Hebrew Documents of the Eighth-Sixth Centuries B.C. II. The Murabba'at Papyrus and the Letter Found near Yabneh-yam." BASOR 165 (1962): 34–46.

603. Delekat, L. "Ein Bittschriftenurf Eines Sabbatschänders (in Meṣad Ḥashavyahu)." Bib 51 (1970): 453–70.

604. Garbini, G. "Note Epigrafiche: 1. Gli ostraka di Kamid el-Loz; 2. L'ostrakon ebraico di Yavneh Yam." AIUON 22 (1972): 95–102.

605. Lemaire, A. "L'Ostracon de Meṣad Ḥashavyahu (Yavneh-Yam) replacé dans son contexte." Sem 21 (1971): 57–79.

606. Michaud, H. "Une Nouvelle Lettre en paleohébraique." VT 10 (1960): 453–55.

607. Naveh, J. "A Hebrew Letter from Meṣad Ḥashavyahu." BIES 25 (1961): 119–28 (Hebrew).

608. ———. "A Hebrew Letter from the Seventh Century B.C." IEJ 10 (1960): 129–39.

609. ———. "More Hebrew Inscriptions from Meṣad Ḥashavyahu." IEJ 12 (1962): 27–31; BIES 27 (1963): 158–64.

610. ———. "Some Notes on the Reading of the Meṣad Ḥashavyahu Letter." IEJ 14 (1964): 158–59.

611. Pardee, D. "A Brief Note on Meṣad Ḥashavyahu Ostracon, 1:12: *w'ml'*." BASOR 239 (1980): 47–48.

612. ———. "The Judicial Plea from Meṣad Ḥashavyahu (Yavneh-Yam): A New Philological Study." *Maarav* 1 (1978): 33–66.

613. Richardson, H. N. "A New Seventh Century Hebrew Ostracon." JBR 29 (1961): 3.

614. Sasson, V. "An Unrecognized Juridical Term in the Yabneh-

Yam Lawsuit and in an Unnoticed Biblical Parallel." BASOR 232 (1978): 57–63.

615. Stefaniak, L. "Sensacyjne Odkrycie Tekstu Hebrajskiego." *Ruch Biblijny i Liturgiczny* 13 (1960): 363–64.

616. Talmon, S. "The New Hebrew Letter from the Seventh Century b.c. in Historical Perspective." BASOR 176 (1964): 29–38.

617. Vattioni, F. "Una lettera ebraica del VII secolo a. C. scoperta à Javne-Jam." *Revista Biblica (Italiana)* 8 (1960): 181–84.

618. Vinnikov, I. N. "O Vnov' Otkrytoj Nadpisi k Jugu ot Jaffy." ArOr 33 (1965): 546–52.

619. Yeivin, S. "The Judicial Petition from Meṣad Ḥashavyahu." BO 19 (1962): 3–10.

The Seal and Impression of "Yirmeyahu." *(Courtesy of the Israel Museum, Jerusalem)*

3

Hebrew Seals

620. Aharoni, Y. "Excavations at Tel Arad." IEJ 17 (1967): 233–47.

621. ———. "Some More *YHWD* Stamps." IEJ 9 (1959): 55–56.

621a. ———. "Three Hebrew Seals." TA 1 (1974): 157–58.

622. ———. "The Use of Hieratic Numerals in Hebrew Ostraca and the Shekel Weights." BASOR 184 (1966): 13–19.

623. Ahituv, S. "Pashḥur." IEJ 20 (1970): 95–96.

624. Albright, W. F. "The Administrative Divisions of Israel and Judah." JPOS 5 (1925): 17–54.

625. ———. "King Joiachin in Exile." BA 5 (1942): 49–55.

626. ———. "The Seal of Eljakim and the Latest Preexilic History of Judah, with Some Observations." JBL 51 (1932): 77–106.

627. Amiran, R., and Eitan, A. "Excavations in the Jerusalem Citadel." In Y. Yadin, ed., *Jerusalem Revealed*. New Haven, Conn., 1975. 52–54.

627a. Avigad, N. "'*ašer 'al hammas.*" Qad 14 (1981): 38–9 (Hebrew): *Beth Mikra* 27 (1981): 1–2.

628. ———. "Baruch the Scribe and Jerahmeel the King's Son." IEJ 28 (1978): 52–56; Qad 11 (1978): 113–14 (Hebrew).

629. ———. *Bullae and Seals from a Post-Exilic Judean Archive.* Kedem Monographs 4. Jerusalem, 1976.

629a. ———. "The Chief of the Corvée." IEJ 30 (1980): 170–73.

630. ———. "Excavations in the Jewish Quarter of the Old City, 1969–1971." In Y. Yadin, ed., *Jerusalem Revealed*. New Haven, Conn., 1975. 41–51; IEJ 20 (1970): 1–8, 129–40; IEJ 22 (1972): 193–200.

631. ———. "Gleanings from Unpublished Ancient Seals." BASOR 230 (1978): 67–69.

632.   ———. "The Governor of the City." IEJ 26 (1976): 178–82; Qad 10 (1977): 68–69 (Hebrew).

633.   ———. "A Group of Hebrew Seals." EI 9 (1969): 1–9, 134 (Hebrew, with English summary on p. 134).

634.   ———. "A Hebrew Seal with a Family Emblem." IEJ 16 (1966): 50–53.

635.   ———. "Jeraḥmeel and Baruch." BA 42 (1979): 114–18.

636.   ———. "The Jotham Seal from Elath." BASOR 163 (1961): 18–22.

637.   ———. "The King's Daughter and the Lyre." IEJ 28 (1978): 146–51; Qad 12 (1979): 61–62 (Hebrew).

638.   ———. "A New Class of Yehud Stamps." IEJ 7 (1957): 146–53; BIES 22 (1958): 3–10.

639.   ———. "New Light on the MṢH Seal Impression." BIES 22 (1958): 126–33; IEJ 8 (1958): 113–19.

640.   ———. "New Names on Hebrew Seals." EI 12 (1975): 66–71 (Hebrew).

641.   ———. "The Priest of Dor." IEJ 25 (1975): 101–7.

642.   ———. "A Sculptured Hebrew Stone Weight." IEJ 18 (1968): 181–87.

643.   ———. "A Seal of a Slave-wife." PEQ 78 (1946): 125–32.

644.   ———. "The Seal of Abigad." IEJ 18 (1968): 52–53.

645.   ———. "The Seal of Jezebel." IEJ 14 (1964): 274–76.

646.   ———. "A Seal of 'Manasseh Son of the King.'" IEJ 13 (1963): 133–36.

647.   ———. "The Seal of 'Seriah ben Neriah.'" EI 14 (1978): 86–87.

647a.   ———. In M. Haran and B. Z. Lurie, joint eds., *Sefer Tur-Sinai*. Jerusalem, 1960. 319–24 (Hebrew). (Seals).

648.   ———. "Seals." In *Encyclopedia Miqra'it*. Jerusalem, 1958. 3: 67–86 (Hebrew).

649.   ———. "Seals and Sealings." IEJ 14 (1964): 190–94.

649a.   ———. "Seals of Exiles." IEJ 15 (1965): 222–32.

650.   ———. "Seven Ancient Hebrew Seals." BIES 18 (1954): 147–53 (Hebrew).

652.   ———. "Six Ancient Hebrew Seals." In S. Abramsky, ed., *Sepher Shmu'el Yeivin*. Jerusalem, 1970. 305–8.

652a.   ———. "Some Hebrew Readings of Hebrew Seals." EI 1 (1951): 32–34 (Hebrew).

653.   ———. "Three Ornamented Hebrew Seals." IEJ 4 (1954): 235–38.

654.   ———. "Titles and Symbols on Hebrew Seals." EI 15 (1981): 303–5.

655. ———. "Two Newly Found Hebrew Seals." IEJ 13 (1963): 322–24.

656. ———. "Two *n'r* Seals." In F. M. Cross et al., eds., *Magnalia Dei, Essays in Memory of George Ernest Wright*. New York, 1976. 294–300.

657. ———. "Unpublished Ancient Seals." BIES 25 (1961): 239–44 (Hebrew).

657a. Barkay, G. "Iron Age Gerah Weights." EI 15 (1981): 288–96 (Hebrew).

658. ———. "A Second Bulla of a *Sar ha-'ir*." Qad 10 (1977): 69–71 (Hebrew).

659. Barnett, R. D. "Hebrew, Palmyrene and Hittite Antiquities." BMQ 14 (1940): 31–32.

660. Barrois, A. "La Métrologie dans la Bible." RB 40 (1931): 209.

661. Barth, J. "Zwei Neuentdeckte Althebräische Siegelinschriften." *Jahrbuch der Jüdischen Literatur Gesellschaft* (1907): 185–90.

662. Bartlett, J. R. "The Seal of *Ḥnh* from the Neighborhood of Tell ed-Duweir." PEQ 108 (1976): 59f.

662a. Barton, G. A. "Three Objects in the Collection of Mr. Herbert Clark of Jerusalem." JAOS 27 (1906): 400.

663. ———. "Two New Hebrew Weights." JAOS 24 (1903): 384ff.

664. Ben, D. A. "The Talmud was Right: The Weight of the Biblical Sheqel." PEQ 100 (1968): 145–47.

664a. Ben-David, A. "The Philistine Talent from Ashdod, the Ugaritic Talent from Ras Shamra, the 'PYM' and the 'N-Ṣ-P.'" UF 11 (1979): 29–45.

665. Ben-Dor, I. "A Hebrew Seal." QDAP 13 (1947–48): 90–91.

666. ———. "A Hebrew Seal in a Gold Signet Ring." BJPES 12 (1945–46): 43–45 (Hebrew).

667. ———. "Two Hebrew Seals." QDAP 13 (1947–48): 64–67.

668. C. Bennett. "Excavations at Buseirah, Southern Jordan." *Levant* 6 (1974): 1–21.

669. Benzinger, I. *Hebräische Archäologie*. 3d ed. Leipzig, 1927. 195ff.

670. Berger, Ph. "Intaille à légende hébraique provenant de Carthage." RA 6 (1906): 83.

670a. ———. "Sur une nouvelle intaille à légende sémitique de la Bibliothèque Nationale." RA 4 (1897): 57f.

671. Bergman, A. "Two Hebrew Seals of the 'Ebed Class." JBL 55 (1936): 224–26.

672. Biran, A., and Cohen, R. "Aroer in the Negev." Qad 11 (1978): 20–24 (Hebrew); IEJ 26 (1976): 139.

673. Blau, O. "Phönikische Analekten." ZDMG 19 (1865): 535.

674. ———. "Review of Levy, Dr. M. A., *Phönizische Studien* (Breslau, 1856)." ZDMG 12 (1858): 726.

675. Bliss, F. J. "Second Report on the Excavations at Tell el-Judeideh." PEQ 33 (1900): 199–222.

676. Bordreuil, P. "Inscriptions sigillaires ouest-sémitiques." *Syria* 50 (1973): 181–95.

677. ———. "Inscriptions sigillaires ouest-sémitiques II." *Syria* 52 (1975): 107–18.

678. ———, and Lemaire, A. "Nouveaux Sceaux hébreux, arameens et ammonites." Sem 26 (1976): 45–63.

679. ———, and Lemaire, A. "Trois Sceaux nord-ouest sémitiques inédits." Sem 24 (1974): 25–34.

680. "List of Cast and Wax Impressions of Stamped Jar-handles Sent to London by Dr. Bliss (April 27th 1900)." PEFQS 32 (1900): 298.

681. Chajes, H. P. "Varia." *Rivista Israelitica* 2 (1905): 146ff.

681a. deClercq, A. R. *Collection de Clercq.* Paris, 1911.

682. Clermont-Ganneau, C. "Antiquities of Palestine in London." PEFQS 16 (1884): 226.

683. ———. "Cachet israélite archaïque aux noms d'Ichmael et Pedayahou." RAO 2 (1899): 251–53.

684. ———. "Cinq Poids israélites à inscriptions." RAO 4 (1901): 26ff.

685. ———. "Deux Alabastra israélites archaiques découverts à Susé." RAO 7 (1904): 294–304.

686. ———. "Fiches et notules: quatre cachets israélites archaïques." RAO 6 (1903): 114ff.

687. ———. "Inscribed Jar-Handles of Palestine." PEFQS 32 (1900): 251ff.

688. ———. "Inscriptions de Palestine." RAO 6 (1903): 173.

689. ———. "Jarres israélites marquées à l'estampille des rois de Juda." RAO 4 (1901): 1–21.

690. ———. "Note on the Inscribed Jar-handles and Weights Found at Tell-Zakariya." PEFQS 31 (1899): 204–9.

691. ———. "Note on Prof. Theodore F. Wright's Inscribed Weight or Bead." PEFQS 25 (1893): 257.

692. ———. "Note sur deux alabastra israélites archaïques découverts à Susé." CRAIBL (1906), 237–48; RAO 7 (1904): 294–304.

693. ———. "Notes on Hebrew and Jewish Inscriptions." PEFQS 23 (1891): 240–43.

693a. ———. "Un Nouveau Cachet israélite archaïque." CRAIBL, ser. 4, 24 (1896): 77.

694.   ———. "Nouvelles Intailles à légendes sémitiques provenant de Palestine." CRAIBL (1892): 274–82; RAO 1 (1898): 36; RAO 6 (1903): 297.

696.   ———. "An Old Hebrew Seal from Deîr Abên," PEFQS 34 (1902): 263ff.

697.   ———. "Quatre Cachets israélites archaïques." RAO 6 (1903): 116ff.

698.   ———. "Quatre Nouveaux Sceaux à légendes sémitiques." RAO 3 (1900): 188f.

698a.   ———. "Le Sceau d' Adoniphelet, serviteur de Amminadab." Études d'Archéologie Orientale 1 (1895): 85–90.

699.   ———. "Le Sceau de Chema, serviteur de Jéroboam." RAO 6 (1903): 294–98.

700.   ———. "Le Sceau d'Obadyahu, fonctionaire royale israélite." RAO 1 (1898): 33–38.

701.   ———. "Sceau israélite au nom d'Abigail, femme de 'Asa-yahon." RAO 3 (1900): 154–56.

702.   ———. "Sceau sémitique." CRAIBL (1909): 333–37.

703.   ———. Sceaux et cachets israélites, phéniciens et syriens, suivis d'épigraphes phéniciennes inédites. . . . Paris, 1883.

704.   ———. "Sceaux et poids à légendes sémitiques du Ashmolean Museum." RAO 4 (1901): 193ff.

704a.   ———. "Sur quelques cachets israélites archaïques." RAO 4 (1901): 255.

705.   ———. "Sur quelques cachets israélites archaïques, II." RAO 4 (1901): 258.

706.   ———. "Sur quelques cachets israélites archaïques, III." RAO 4 (1901): 259.

707.   ———. "Three New Archaic Israelite Seals." PEFQS 34 (1902): 264–68.

708.   ———. "Trois Nouveaux Cachets israélites archaïques." RAO 5 (1902): 125.

708a.   Colella, P. "Baruch lo scriba e Jerahmeel il figlio del re." BeO 23 (1981): 87–96.

708b.   Conder, C. R. "The Seal of Haggai." PEFQS 22 (1890): 121f.

709.   Cook, S. A. "Inscribed Jar-handles." PEFQS 57 (1925): 91ff.

710.   ———. "Miscellaneous Notes." PEFQS 61 (1929): 61–62.

711.   ———. "Newly-Discovered Hebrew Seal." PEFQS 36 (1904): 287–91.

712.   ———. "Notes and Queries." PEFQS 41 (1909): 232.

713.   ———. "Notes on Excavations." PEFQS 61 (1929): 111–18.

714.   ———. "Notes on Semitic Inscriptions." PSBA 26 (1904): 109ff. 164–65.

715.   ———. "Notes on Semitic Inscriptions, III, 3. Personal Names on Hebrew Intaglios." PSBA 26 (1904): 166.

716.   ———. "Notices of Publications." PEFQS 61 (1929): 123.

717.   ———. "Reviews and Notices of Publications (of *Journal of the German Palestinian Society* 37)." PEFQS 46 (1914): 154.

718.   Cross, F. M. "An Archaic Inscribed Seal from the Valley of Aijalon." BASOR 168 (1962): 12–18.

719.   ———. "Judean Stamps." EI 9 (1969): 20–27.

720.   Dalman, G. "Ein Neugefundenes Jahvebild." PJB 2 (1906): 46.

720a.   ———. "Neugefundene Gewichte." ZDPV 29 (1906): 92ff.

721.   Davis, D., and Kloner, A. "A Burial Cave of the Late Israelite Period on the Slopes of Mt. Zion." Qad 2 (1978): 16–19 (Hebrew).

722.   Delaporte, L. *Catalogue des Cylindres*. Paris, 1923.

723.   DeLongperier, A. "Cachet de Sébénias, fils d'Osias." CRAIBL 6 (1863): 288; RA, n.s. 4 (1863): 358ff.

724.   DeVogue, M. "Intailles à légendes sémitiques." RA (1868), 436f.

725.   Diringer, D. "The Royal Jar-Handle Stamps of Ancient Judah." BA 12 (1949): 70–86.

727.   ———. "Three Early Hebrew Seals." ArOr 18/3 (1950): 65–68.

728.   Driver, G. R. "Hebrew Seals." PEQ 87 (1955): 183.

729.   ———. "Seals and Tombstones." ADAJ 2 (1953): 62–65.

730.   Friedmann, K. "Le fonti per la storia dagli ebrei di Cirenacia nell' antichità." In E. S. Artom, U. Cassuto, I. Zoller, eds., *Miscellanea di studi ebraici in memoria di H. P. Chajes*. Florence, 1930.

731.   Fulco, W. J. "A Seal from Umm el-Qanafid, Jordan: *g'lyhw 'bd hmlk*." Or 48 (1979): 107–8.

732.   Galling, K. Archäologischer Jahresbericht." ZDPV 52 (1929): 249ff.

733.   ———. "Beschriftete Bildsiegel des I. Jahrtausends v. Chr. vornehmlich aus Syrien und Palästina." ZDPV 64 (1941): 121–202.

734.   ———. "Ein Hebräisches Siegel aus der Babylonischen Diaspora." ZDPV 51 (1928): 234–36.

734a.   ———. "Das Siegel des Jotham von Tell el-Hlefi." ZDPV 83 (1967): 131–34.

735.   Giron, M. N. "Notes épigraphiques." JA 11, 19–20 (1922), 63–65.

736.   ———. "Notes épigraphiques, 2. deux cachets hébraiques." *Mélanges de la Faculté Orientale de Beyrouth* 5 (1911): 75f.

737. Giveon, R. "Two New Hebrew Seals and Their Iconographic Background." PEQ 93 (1961): 38–42.

738. Glueck, N. Note in "Archaeological Work in Palestine and Syria During 1932." BASOR 49 (1933): 17.

738a. ———. "A Seal Weight from Nebi Rubin." BASOR 153 (1959): 35–38.

738b. Görg, M. "Die Königstochter und die Leier." BN 14 (1981): 7–10.

739. Graessner, C. "The Seal of Elijah." BASOR 220 (1975): 63–66.

740. Gressmann, H. *Altorientalische Bilder*. Berlin, 1927.

741. ———. "Die Ausgrabungen in Palästina und das Alte Testament." *Religionsgeschichtliche Volksbücher für die Deutsche Christliche Gegenwart*, ser. 3, 10: 42–43, 46.

742. ———. "Bemerkungen des Herausgebers." ZAW, n.s. 1 (1924): 347.

743. ———. "Wichtige Zeitschriften-Aufsätze." ZAW, n.s. 3 (1926): 159.

744. ———. "Zeitschriftenaufsätze," ZAW, n.s. 2 (1925): 239, 294ff.

745. Halevy, J. "Notes et mélanges. Sceau hébreu en forme scaraboide." RS 9 (1901): 263.

746. Harding, G. L. "Four Tomb Groups from Jordan." PEFA 6 (1953): 1–70.

747. ———. "Some Objects from Transjordan." PEQ 69 (1937): 253–55.

747a. Herr, L. G. "Paleography and the Identification of Seal Owners." BASOR 239 (1980): 67–70.

748. ———. *The Scripts of Ancient Northwest Semitic Seals*. Missoula, Mont., 1978.

749. Hestrin, R., and Dayagi, M. *Inscribed Seals, First Temple Period*. Jerusalem, 1979.

750. ———. *Israel Museum News* 12 (1977): 75–77 (seals in the Israel Museum Collection).

751. ———. "A Seal Impression of a 'servant' ('Ebed) of King Hezekiah." Qad 7/3–4 (1974): 104ff. (Hebrew); IEJ 24 (1974): 27–29.

752. Hitzig, F. "Epigraphische Miscellen." ZDMG 12 (1858): 698.

753. Horn, S. H. "An Inscribed Seal from Jordan." BASOR 189 (1968): 41–43.

754. ———. "A Seal from Amman." BASOR 205 (1972): 43–45.

755. Irwin, W. A. "An Ancient Biblical Text." AJSL 48 (1931/32): 184–93.

The Seal and Impression of "Shafaṭ." *(Courtesy of the Israel Museum, Jerusalem)*

756. Juda, A. C. *Études demonstratives de la langue phénicienne et de la langue libyque*. Paris, 1847.

757. Kautzsch, E. "Ein Althebräisches Siegel." MNDPV 10 (1904): 1ff.

758. ———. "Zur Deutung des Löwen-siegels." MNDPV 10 (1904): 82–83.

759. Klein, S. "*lyqm*, Servant of *ywkn*." BIES 5 (1938): 98–101 (Hebrew).

759a. Kochavi, M. In Y. Aharoni, ed., *Excavations and Studies, Essays in Honor of S. Yeivin*. Tel Aviv, 1973. 49–75 (Hebrew) (sealings from Khirket Rabud).

760. König, G. "The Haematite Weight with an Inscription in Ancient Semitic Characters, Purchased at Samaria in 1890 by Thomas Chaplin, Esq. M.D. (The Academy, 4 November, 1893)." PEFQS 26 (1894): 222–24.

761. Kutscher, Y. "Two Hebrew Seals." *Kedem* 1 (1942): 44–45.

762. Lance, H. D. "The Royal Stamps and the Kingdom of Josiah." HThR 64 (1971): 315–32.

763. Lane, W. R. "Newly Recognized Occurrences of the Weight-Name *PYM*." BASOR 164 (1961): 21.

764. Lapp, P. W. "Late Royal Seals from Judah." BASOR 158 (1960): 11–22.

765. ———. "Ptolemaic Stamped Handles from Judah." BASOR 172 (1963): 22–35.

766. Ledrain, E. "Notes sur deaux sceaux portant le même nom hébreu." RA, n.s. 43 (1882): 285–87.

766a. Lemaire, A. "Classification des estampilles royales judéennes." EI 15 (1981): 54–60.

766b. ———. "Note sur le titre *bn hmlk* dans l'ancien Israel." Sem 29 (1979): 59–65.

767. ———. "Remarques sur la datation des estampilles *lmlk*," VT 25 (1975): 678–82.

768. Levy, I. "Notes d'histoire et d'épigraphie, I. Cachet d'Ouzziahou, fils de Hareph." REJ 41 (1900): 174.

769. ———. "Notes d'histoire et d'épigraphie, II. *hwrtz* et *pqll*." REJ 41 (1900): 175.

770. Levy, M. A. "Althebräische Siegelsteine." ZDMG 11 (1857): 318–24.

771. ———. *Siegel und Gemmen mit Aramäischen, Phönizischen, Althebräischen, Himjarischen, Nabathäischen und Altsyrischen Inschriften Erklärt*. Breslau, 1869.

772. Lidzbarski, M. "Notes." PEFQS 39 (1907): 78–79.

773. ———. "Notes." PEFQS 40 (1908): 76–77.

774. Luckenbill, D. D. "Azariah of Judah." AJSL 41 (1924–25): 217–32.

775. Macalister, R. A. S. "Alphabet of Letters Used on Old-Hebrew Jar-Seals." PEFQS 32 (1900): 341.

776. ———. "Another Old Hebrew Jar-Seal." PEFQS 41 (1909): 22.

777. ———. "The Craftsmen's Guild of the Tribe of Judah." PEFQS 37 (1905): 243–53, 328–42; PEFQS 40 (1908): 71–75.

778. ———. "Potters' Stamps and Other Seals." PEFQS 36 (1904): 211–14.

779. Martin, M. F. "Six Palestinian Seals." RSO 39 (1964): 203–10.

780. May, H. G. "Seal of Elamar." AJSL 52 (1935/36): 197–99.

781. ———. "Three Hebrew Seals and the Status of Exiled Jehoiakin." AJSL 56 (1939): 146–48.

781a. Mazar, B. BIES 26 (1962): 57 (Seals from En Gedi).

782. ———, et al., "The Excavations at Tell Goren (Tell el-Jurn) in 1961–1962," Atiqot 5 (1966): 37–38.

783. ———. *The Mountain of the Lord*. New York, 1975. 179.

784. Meshel, Z. "Kuntilat 'Ajrud, 1975–1976." IEJ 27 (1977): 52–53.

785. Moscati, S. "I sigilli nell' Antico Testamento." Bib 30 (1949): 314–38.

786. Na'aman, N. "Sennacharib's Campaign to Judah and the Date of the *lmlk* Stamps." VT 29 (1979): 61–86.

787. Naveh, J. "Old Aramaic Inscriptions (1960–1965)." *Leshonenu* 29 (1965): 185 (Hebrew).

788. ———. "Canaanite and Hebrew Inscriptions (1960–1964)." *Leshonenu* 30 (1966): 65–68 (Hebrew).

789. ———. "Two Hebrew Seals." Qad 1 (1968): 105 (Hebrew).

790. O'Connell, K. G. "An Israelite Bulla from Tell el-Hesi." IEJ 27 (1977): 197–99.

791. Petrie, W. M. F. *Ancient Weights and Measures*. London, 1926.

791a. ———. *Gerar*. London, 1928. Pl. 43.1.

792. ———. *Measures and Weights*. London, 1934.

793. ———. *Scarabs and Cylinders with Names*. London, 1917.

793a. Pilcher, E. J. "Bronze Weight from Petra," PEFQS 54 (1922): 71–73.

794. ———. "The Jewish Royal Pottery Stamps." PSBA 33 (1910): 93–101, 143–52.

794a. ———. "A New Hebrew Weight." PEFQS 47 (1915): 40ff.

795. ———. "Signet of Hananiah." PEFQS 55 (1923): 94–97.

796. ———. "Signet with Old-Hebrew Inscription." PEFQS 51 (1919): 177–81.

797. ———. "Weights of Ancient Palestine." PEFQS 44 (1912): 136–44, 178–95.

798. ———. "Weight Standards of Palestine." PSBA 34 (1912): 114f.

799. Porada, E. *Corpus of Ancient Near Eastern Seals in North American Collections.* Washington, 1948.

800. Porten, B. *"Domla'el* and Related Names." IEJ 21 (1971): 47–49.

801. Pottier, E. "Communication." CRAIBL (1904), 336–38.

801a. Raffaeli, S. "Two Ancient Hebrew Weights." JPOS 1 (1920): 22ff.

802. Rahmani, L. I. "A Hebrew Seal from Horbat Shovav." *Atiqot* 5 (1969): 81–83 (Hebrew).

803. Rainey, A. F. "Private Seal Impressions: A Note on Semantics." IEJ 16 (1966): 187–90.

803a. ———. "Royal Weights and Measures." BASOR 179 (1965): 34–35.

804. Read, F. W. "The Persian and Egyptian Affinities of the Jewish Royal Pottery Stamps." PEFQS 42 (1910): 232ff.

805. Reifenberg, A. *Ancient Hebrew Seals.* London, 1950.

806. ———. "Ancient Jewish Stamps and Seals." PEQ 72 (1939): 193–95.

807. ———. "Discovery of a New Hebrew Inscription of the Pre-Exilic Period." BJPES 13 (1947): 80–83.

808. ———. "Hebrew Seals and Stamps IV." IEJ 4 (1954): 139–42.

809. ———. "The Legend 'Shekel' on Hebrew Weights." BJPES 15 (1949): 70 (Hebrew).

809a. ———. "Ein Neues Hebräisches Gewicht." JPOS 16 (1936): 39–43.

810. ———. "Some Ancient Hebrew Seals." PEQ 71 (1938): 113–16.

811. ———. "Some Ancient Hebrew Seals II." PEQ 72 (1939): 195–98.

812. ———. "Some Ancient Hebrew Seals III." PEQ 74 (1942): 109–112.

813. Richardson, H. N. "A Stamped Handle from Khirbet Yarmuk." BASOR 192 (1968): 12–16.

814. Robertson-Smith, W. "The Haematite Weight with an Inscription in Ancient Semitic Character, Purchased at Samaria in 1890 by Thomas Chaplin, Esq. M.D." The Academy, 18 November 1893. PEFQS 26 (1894): 225–31.

815. Rödiger, E. "Ein Dritter Hebräischer Siegelstein." ZDMG 3 (1849): 347–48.

816. Ronzevalle, S. "Intailles orientales." *Mélanges de la Faculté Orientale de Beyrouth* 7 (1914–21): 186ff.

816a. Sauer, G. "Siegel." In B. Reicke, ed., *Biblisch-historisches Handwörterbuch*, vol. 3. Göttingen, 1966, cols. 1786–90.

817. Sayce, A. H. "The Age of the Inscribed Jar-Handles from Palestine." PEFQS 32 (1900): 66ff.

818. ———. "The Early Jewish Inscriptions on H. Clark's Seals." PEFQS 41 (1909): 155.

819. ———. "Hebrew Inscriptions of the Preexilic Period. *The Academy*, 2 August 1890.

820. ———. "The Jar-Handles Found by Dr. Bliss." PEFQS 32 (1900): 170.

821. ———. "On an Inscribed Bead from Palestine." PEFQS 25 (1893): 32ff.

822. Sarfatti, G. B. "Notes on the Inscriptions on Some Jewish Coins and Seals." IEJ 27 (1977): 204–6.

823. Schick, C. "Neue Ausgrabungen der Englischen Palästina Gesellschaft." MNDPV 1 (1899): 14ff.

824. Schröder, P. "Vier Siegelsteine mit Semitischen Legenden, 1. Althebräischer Siegelstein." ZDPV 37 (1914): 172ff; ZDPV 38 (1915): 154ff.

826. Scott, R. B. Y. "The *N-Ṣ-P* Weights from Judah." BASOR 200 (1970): 62–66.

827. ———. "The Seal of *šmryw*." VT 14 (1964): 108–10.

828. ———. "Shekel Fraction Markings on Hebrew Weights." BASOR 173 (1964): 53–64.

829. ———. "The Shekel Sign on Stone Weights." BASOR 153 (1959): 32–35.

830. ———. "Weights and Measures of the Bible." BA 22 (1959): 22–40.

830a. Segal, M. H. "A New Hebrew Weight." PEFQS 47 (1915): 40f.

831. Sellers, D. R. *The Citadel of Beth-Zur*. Philadelphia, 1933. 60–61.

832. ———, and Albright, W. F. "The First Campaign of Excavation at Beth-zur." BASOR 43 (1939): 1–13.

833. Sellin, E. "Die in Palästina Ausgegrabenen Altisraelitischen Krugstempel." *Neue Kirchliche Zeitschrift* 17 (1907): 753–63.

833a. Shany, E. "A New Unpublished *Beq'a* Weight in the Collection of the Pontifical Biblical Institute, Jerusalem, Israel." PEQ 99 (1967): 54–55.

834. Shiloh, Y. "City of David Excavation 1978." BA 42 (1979): 165–71.

835. ———, and Kaplan, M. "Digging in the City of David." BAR 5 (1979): 36–49.

835a. Spaer, A. "A Group of Iron Age Stone Weights." IEJ 32 (1982): 251.

836. Speiser, E. A. "Of Shoes and Shekels." BASOR 77 (1940): 15–20.

838. Stade, B. "Vier im Jahre 1896 Publizierte Altsemitische Siegelsteine." ZAW 17 (1897): 204–6.

839. Stieglitz, R. R. "The Seal of *Ma'aśyahu*." IEJ 23 (1973): 236–37.

840. Sukenik, E. L. "A Further Note on Hebrew Seals." *Kedem* 1 (1942): 46.

841. ———. "Gleanings." *Kedem* 1 (1942): 94–96.

842. ———. "An Israelite Gem from Samaria." PEFQS 60 (1928), 51.

843. ———. "The Meaning of the '*Le-Melekh*' Inscriptions." *Kedem* 1 (1942): 32–36.

844. ———. "A Note on the Seal of the Servant of Ahaz." BASOR 84 (1941): 17–19, with postscript by W. F. Albright.

845. ———. "A Seal of the Servant of King Ahaz." *Kedem* 1 (1942): 94–95.

846. ———. "Three Ancient Seals." *Kedem* 2 (1943): 8–10.

846a. Tadmor, H. "A Note on the Seal of Mannuki-Inurta." IEJ 15 (1965): 233.

847. Torrey, C. C. "A Few Ancient Seals." AASOR 2 (1923): 103–8.

848. ———. "A Hebrew Seal From the Reign of Ahaz." BASOR 79 (1940): 27–29, with postscript by W. F. Albright.

849. ———. "An Inscribed Hebrew Weight." JAOS 24 (1903): 206–8.

850. ———. "Notes on a Few Inscriptions, B. The 'Ankh' Symbol on Hebrew Seals." JAOS 29 (1908): 192–203.

851. ———. "The Seal From the Reign of Ahaz Again." BASOR 82 (1941): 16–17, with postscripts by W. F. Albright and C. C. Torrey.

852. ———. "Semitic Epigraphical Notes I. An Old Hebrew Seal." JAOS 24 (1903): 205–6.

853. Tufnell, O. "Seals and Scarabs." *Interpreter's Dictionary of the Bible*. Nashville, Tenn., (1976), 4: 254–59.

854. Tushingham, A. D. "A Royal Israelite Seal (?) and the Royal Jar Handle Stamps." BASOR 200 (1970): 71–78; BASOR 201 (1971): 23–35.

855. Ussishkin, D. "Royal Judean Storage Jars and Private Seal Impressions." BASOR 223 (1976): 1–13.

856. Vattioni, F. "I sigilli ebraici." Bib 50 (1969): 357–88.

857. ———. "I sigilli ebraici II." *Augustinianum* 11 (1971): 447–54.

858. deVaux, R. "Le Sceau de Godolias, maître du palais." RB 45 (1936): 66–102.

858a. Veenhof, K. R. "Nieuwe Aramese Inscriptes." Phoenix 16 (1968): 132–42.

859. Vincent, L. H. "Un Nouveau Cachet israélite," RB, n.s. 7 (1910): 417.

860. ———. "Une Nouvelle Estampille judéo-araméenne." RB 19 (1910): 578.

861. ———. "Nouvelle Intaille israélite," RB 11 (1902): 435ff.

862. ———. "Pseudo-figure de Jahve, récemment mise en circulation." RB, n.s. 6 (1909): 121–27.

863. Welten, P. *Die Königs-Stemple. Ein Beitrag zur Militärpolitik Judas unter Hiskia und Josia.* Wiesbaden, 1969.

863a. "What Did David's Lyre Look Like?" BAR 8/1 (1982): 34–5.

864. Wright, G. E. "Archaeological News and Views." BA 12 (1949): 91–92.

865. ———. "*Qosanal,* Servant of the King." BA 1 (1938): 16.

866. ———. "Some Personal Seals of Judean Royal Officials." BA 1 (1938): 10–12.

867. Wright, Th. F. "Jar-Handle Inscriptions." PEFQS 33 (1901): 60ff.

868. ———. "Jar-Handles." *Biblical World* 17 (1901): 135ff.

869. Yadin, Y. "The Fourfold Division of Judah." BASOR 163 (1961): 6–12; IEJ 18 (1968): 50–51.

870. ———. "A Hebrew Seal from Tell Jemmeh." EI 6 (1960): 53–55 (Hebrew).

871. Yeivin, S. "The Date of the Seal of *Shema,* Servant of Jeroboam." EI 6 (1960): 47–52; JNES 19 (1960): 205–12.

872. ———. "Epigraphic Notes on the Seal of *Ma'asayahu/ Yesha'yahu.*" EI 12 (1975): 81f.

872a. ———. "To N. Avigad's Article 'The Princess and the Lyre' [Qad 12 (1979): 61-2]." Qad 13 (1980): 56 (Hebrew).

872b. Zeron, A. "The Seal of 'M-B-N' and the List of David's Heroes." TA 6 (1979): 156–7.

873. Zoller, I. "Syrisch-Palästinensische Altertümer." MGWJ 72 (1928): 230, 235ff.

The Seal and Impression of "Hym." *(Courtesy of the Israel Department of Antiquities and Museums)*

4

Miscellaneous

873a. Angerstorfer, A. "Ašerah als 'consort of Jahwe' oder Aštirah." BN 17 (1982): 7–16.

874. Avigad, N. "Another *bat le-melekh* Inscription." IEJ 3 (1953): 121–22.

875. ———. "Two Hebrew Inscriptions on Wine Jars." IEJ 22 (1972): 1–9.

876. ———. "*Yehud* or *Ha'ir?*" BASOR 158 (1960): 23–27.

877. Bachi, R. "Ricordi ebraici in Macerata." *Israel: La Rassegna Mensile* 8 (1933): 300–303.

877a. Baedeker, C. *Palästina und Syrien.* Leipzig, 1900.

878. Bar-Adon, P. "An Early Hebrew Inscription in a Judean Desert Cave." IEJ 25 (1975): 226–32; EI 12 (1975): 77–80.

879. ———. "An Extended Settlement of the Judean Desert Sect at Ain el-Guweir on the Shore of the Dead Sea." EI 10 (1971): 72–89 (Hebrew).

880. ———. "A Hebrew Inscription of the Judean Monarchy Period from the Judean Desert." Qad 8 (1975): 21–23 (Hebrew).

881. Barkay, G. "A Group of Iron Age Scale Weights." IEJ 28 (1978): 209–17.

882. Bennett, C. "Fouilles d'Umm el-Biyara." RB 73 (1966): 399–401.

883. Benoit, P., Milik, J. T., and deVaux, R. *Discoveries in the Judean Desert II. Les Grottes de Murabba'at.* Oxford, 1961.

883a. Biale, D. "The God With Breasts: El Shaddai in the Bible." *History of Religions* 20 (1982): 241–56.

884. Biraghi, L. *Antica epigrafe ebraica della Cattedra di S. Marco in Venezia.* Milan, 1853.

884a. Bruston, Ch. *Études phéniciennes*. Paris, 1903.

884b. Catastini, A. "Le Iscrizioni di Kuntillet 'Ajrud e il profetismo." *Annali* 42 (1982): 127–34.

885. Chwolson, D. "Die Quiescentes *hwy* in der Althebraeischen Orthographie." *Travaux de la troisième session du Congrès International des Orientalistes, St. Pétersbourg 1876, II.* St. Petersburg and Leiden, 1879. 457–90.

886. Ciprotti, P. "Die Graffiti." *Das Altertum* 13 (1967): 85–94.

886a. Cohen, R. "Did I Excavate Kadesh-Barnea?" BAR 7/3 (1981): 20–33.

887. Cross, F. M. "Two Notes on Palestinian Inscriptions of the Persian Age." BASOR 193 (1969): 19–24.

888. Degen, R., and Müller, W. W. "Eine Hebräisch-Sabäische Bilinguis aus Bait al-Aswal." NESE 2 (1974): 117–24.

889. Diringer, D., and Brock, S. P. "Words and Meanings in Early Hebrew Inscriptions." In *Words and Meanings. Essays Presented to D. Winton Thomas*. Cambridge, 1968, 39–45.

889a. Dotan, A. "New Light on the 'Izbet Ṣarṭah Ostracon." TA 8 (1981): 160–72.

890. Dothan, M. "The Excavations at Tell Mul in 1959." BIES 24 (1960): 120–32 (Hebrew).

890a. Emerton, J. A. "New Light on Israelite Religion: The Implications of Inscriptions from Kuntillet 'Ajrud." ZAW 94 (1982): 2–20.

891. Euting, J. "Epigraphische Miscellen." *Sitzungsberichte der Preussischen Akademie der Wissenschaften* 2 (1885): 667–68.

892. ———. "Notulae epigraphicae. Etiquette hébraique de Momie." *Florilegium M. deVogué*. Paris, 1909. 235–36.

893. Garner, G. G. "Kuntillet 'Ajrud: An Intriguing Site in Sinai," BurH 14/2 (1978): 1–16.

894. Gibson, J. C. L. "Stress and Vocalic Change in Hebrew: A Diachronic Study," JL 2 (1966): 35–56.

895. Ginsberg, H. L. "*MMST* and *MṢH*," BASOR 109 (1948): 20–22.

896. Goitein, S. D. "A Bilingual Himyarite-Hebrew Inscription." *Tarbiz* 41 (1972): 151–56 (Hebrew).

897. Gordis, R. "The Asseverative Kaph in Ugaritic and Hebrew." JAOS 63 (1943): 176–78.

898. Grintz, J. M. "Jehoezer—Unknown High Priest?" JQR 50 (1959–60): 338–45.

899. Heltzer, M. L. "Eighth Century B.C. Inscriptions from Kalakh (Nimrud)." PEQ 110 (1978): 3–9.

899a. Herr, L. G. "The Formal Scripts of Iron Age Transjordan." BASOR 238 (1980): 21–34.

900. Hirshberg, H. Z. "Three Comments on Three Articles in 'Tarbiz 41–42.'" *Tarbiz* 42 (1973): 200–201 (Hebrew).

901. Inge, C. H. "Post-Scriptum (On Ancient Hebrew Inscriptions)." PEQ 73 (1941): 106–9.

902. Isserlin, B. S. J. "Some Archaeological News from Israel." PEQ 82 (1950): 92–101.

903. Kaplan, J. "The Identification of Abel-Beth-Maacah and Janoah." IEJ 28 (1978): 157–60.

903a. King, P. J. "The Contribution of Archaeology to Biblical Studies." CBQ 45 (1983): 1–16.

904. Khvolson, D. A. *Sbornik evreiskikh nadpisei.* St. Petersburg, 1884.

905. Kochavi, M. "Communication de M. Kochavi." RB 72 (1965): 548–51.

906. Lemaire, A. "Note épigraphique sur la pseudo-attestation du mois *sḥ*" VT 23 (1973): 243–45.

906a. Lemaire, A., and Vernus, P. "Les Ostraca paléo-hébreux de Qadesh-Barnea." Or 49 (1980): 341–5.

907. Lemaire, A. "L'Ostracon 'Ramat-Négeb' et la topographie historique du Négeb." Sem 23 (1973): 11–26.

908. ———. "A propos d'une inscription de Tel 'Amal." RB 80 (1973): 559.

908a. Lohfink, N. "Wandkritzeleien aus der Israelitischen Konigszeit." *Stimmen der Zeit* 87 (1961/62): 390–92.

909. Mazar, B. "En Gedi." IEJ 12 (1962): 145–46.

910. ———. "En Gev: Excavations in 1961." IEJ 14 (1964): 27–29.

910a. ———; Dothan, T.; and Dunayevski, E. "En Gedi: The First and Second Seasons of Excavations, 1961–1962." *Atiqot* 5 (1966).

910b. Mazar, B. "A Hebrew Inscription from 'Illar." BIES 18 (1954): 154–57.

910c. McCarter, P. K. "The Balaam Texts from Deir 'Allā: The First Combination." BASOR 239 (1980): 49–60.

911. Meshel, Z. "Did Yahweh Have a Consort?" BAR 5 (1979): 24–35.

912. ———. "Kuntillet 'Ajrud." *Le Monde de la Bible* (Aug.–Oct. 1979), 32–36.

912a. ———. *Kuntillet 'Ajrud; A Religious Centre from the Time of the Judaean Monarchy on the Border of Sinai.* Jerusalem, 1978.

913. ———. "Kuntilat 'Ajrud, 1975–1976." IEJ 27 (1977): 52–53.

913a. ———, and Meyers, C. "The Name of God in the Wilderness of Zin." BA 39 (1976): 6.

914. Millard, A. R. "Alphabetic Inscriptions on Ivories from Nimrud." *Iraq* 24 (1962): 41–51.

915. Mirski, A. "22 Signs in Writing; 22 Sounds." *Leshonenu* 24 (1973): 215–23 (Hebrew).

916. Mittwoch, E. "Hebräische Inschriften aus Palmyra." AA 4 (1902): 203–6.

917. Naveh, J. "Hebrew Texts in Aramaic Script in the Persian Period?" BASOR 203 (1971): 27–32.

918. Negev, A. "Inscriptions hébraiques, grecques et latines de Cesaree Maritime." RB 78 (1971): 247–63.

919. Neubauer, A. "Die Firkowitz'sche Sammlung." Akademiya nank. *Mélanges Asiatiques* 5 (1864): 121–27.

920. Nordio, M. "Iscrizioni ebraiche su due steli giudeo-cristiane di Khirbet Kilkis." AIUON 35 (1975): 179–200.

921. Perrot, J. "Découvertes récentes en Palestine." *Syria* 26 (1949): 155–57; *Syria* 27 (1950): 188–96.

921a. Petrie, W. M. F. *Beth-Pelet I.* London, 1930.

921b. Puech, E. "Abécédaire et liste alphabétique de noms hébreaux du debut du IIe s. A.D." RB 87 (1980): 118–126.

921c. Saller, S. L. *Excavations at Bethany.* Jerusalem, 1957.

922. de Saulcy, F. "Note sur les inscriptions hébraiques de Kefer-Bere'im." Rev Arch (1865): 69–73.

923. Sayce, A. H. *La Lumière nouvelle, traduit par L'abbé Trochon.* Paris, 1888.

924. T. Schrire. *Hebrew Amulets: Their Decipherment and Interpretation.* London, 1966.

925. Sobernheim, M. "Eine Hebräisch-Arabische Inschrift in Aleppo." In G. Weil, ed., *Festschrift Eduard Sachau.* Berlin, 1915. 211–313.

925a. Spaer, A. "A Coin of Jeroboam." IEJ 29 (1979): 218.

926. Staples, W. E. "A Note on an Inscribed Potsherd." PEQ 69 (1936): 155.

927. Sukenik, E. L. "The Earliest Records of Christianity." AJA (1947), 351–65.

928. Testa, E. *Herodion. IV. I graffiiti e gli ostraka. Pubbl. d. Studium Biblicum Franciscanum* 20. Jerusalem, 1972.

929. ———. *L'Huile de la foi. Traduit et adapté de l'italien par Omer Engelbert.* Jerusalem, 1967.

930. Tzori, N. "A Spindle Whorl with Hebrew Inscription." IEJ 9 (1959): 191–92.

931. deVaux, R. "Fouilles au Khirbet Qumran, deuxième campagne." RB 61 (1954): 206–36.

932. Veenhof, K. R. "Balans der Elefantine Papyri, I." *Phoenix* 18 (1970): 305, 310–27.

933. Vincent, L. H. "Notes épigraphiques." RB 11 (1902): 436–37.

934. Vogt, E. "Ostracon Hebraicum saec. 7 a.C." Bib 41 (1960), 183–84.

934a. Weippert, H. and M. "Die 'Bileam'-Inschrift von Tell Dēr 'Allā." ZDPV 98 (1982): 77–103.

935. Winnett, F., and Reed, W. *Ancient Records from North Arabia.* Toronto, 1970.

The Tell Siran Bottle Inscription. *(Courtesy of the Department of Antiquities of Jordan)*

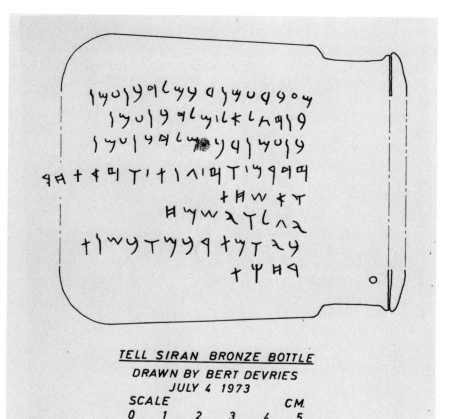

TELL SIRAN BRONZE BOTTLE
DRAWN BY BERT DEVRIES
JULY 4 1973

Drawing of the Tell Siran Bottle Inscription.
(Courtesy of the Department of Antiquities of Jordan)

5
Ammonite Inscriptions

936. Aharoni, Y. "A New Ammonite Inscription." IEJ 1 (1950–51): 219–22.

937. Albright, W. F. "Notes on Ammonite History." In *Miscellanea Biblica B. Ubach*. Vol. 1. Montserrat, 1953.

938. ———. "Some Comments on the 'Amman Citadel Inscription." BASOR 198 (1970): 38–40.

939. Avigad, N. "Ammonite and Moabite Seals." In J. A. Sanders, ed., *Near Eastern Archaeology in the Twentieth Century*. Garden City, N.Y., 1970. 284–95.

940. ———. "An Ammonite Seal." IEJ 2 (1952): 163–64.

941. ———. "Two Ammonite Seals Depicting the *Dea Nutrix*." BASOR 225 (1977): 63–66.

941a. Baldacci, M. "The Ammonite Text from Tell Siran and North-West Semitic Philology." VT 31 (1981): 363–68.

941b. Becking, B. E. J. H. "Zur Interpretation der ammonitischen Inschrift vom Tell Siran." BO 38 (1981): 273–6.

942. Bordreuil, P. "Inscriptions des têtes à double face." ADAJ 18 (1973): 37–39.

943. ———. "Inscriptions sigillaires ouestsémitiques; épigraphie ammonite." *Syria* 50 (1973): 181–95.

943a. Clermont-Ganneau, C. RAO 2 (1899): 45 (Ammonite Seal).

943b. Coote, R. B. "The Tell Siran Bottle Inscription." BASOR 240 (1980): 93.

944. Cross, F. M. "Ammonite Ostraca from Heshbon. Heshbon Ostraca IV–VIII." AUSS 13/1 (1975): 1–20.

945. ———. "Epigraphic Notes on the Amman Citadel Inscription." BASOR 193 (1969): 2–19.

946.   ———. "Leaves from an Epigraphist's Notebook, #3. A Forgotten Seal." CBQ 36 (1974): 486–94.

947.   ———. "Notes on the Ammonite Inscription from Tell Siran." BASOR 212 (1973): 12–15.

948.   Driver, G. R. "Seals from Amman." QDAP 11 (1944): 81–82.

949.   Fulco, W. J. "The 'Amman Citadel Inscription: A New Collation." BASOR 230 (1978): 39–44.

950.   ———. "The Amman Theater Inscription." JNES 38 (1979): 37–38.

951.   Garbini, G. "Ammonite Inscriptions." JSS 19 (1974): 159–68.

952.   ———. "La lingua degli ammoniti." AIUON 30, n.s. 20 (1970): 249–62.

952a.   ———. "Un nuovo sigillo aramaico-ammonita." AIUON 17 (1967): 233–34.

953.   Hammond, P. C. "An Ammonite Stamp Seal from Amman." BASOR 160 (1960): 38–41.

954.   Horn, S. H. "The Amman Citadel Inscription." BASOR 193 (1969): 2–13. ADAJ 12–13 (1967–68): 81–83.

955.   ———. "An Inscribed Seal from Jordan." BASOR 189 (1968): 41.

956.   ———. "A Seal from Amman," BASOR 205 (1972): 43–45.

956a.   Israel, F. "L'Iscrizione di Tell Siran e le Bibbia: la titolatura del sovrano ammonita." BeO 22 (1980): 283–87.

957.   ———. "The Language of the Ammonites." OLP 10 (1979): 143–59.

958.   ———. "Un nuovo sigillo ammonita?" BeO 111–12. (1977): 167–70.

959.   Kutscher, R. "A New Inscription from Amman." Qad 5 (1972): 27–28 (Hebrew).

960.   Landes, G. M. "The Material Culture of the Ammonites." BA 24 (1961): 66–86.

961.   Loretz, O. "Die Ammonitische Inschrift von Tell Siran." UF 9 (1977): 169–71.

961a.   Naveh, J. "The Ostracon form Nimrud: An Ammonite Name-List." *Maarav* 2 (1980): 163–71.

962.   Oded, B. "The Amman Theater Inscription." RSO 44 (1969): 187–89.

963.   Palmaitis, L. "The First Ancient Ammonite Inscription of the I Millennium B.C." VDI 118/4 (1971): 119–26.

964.   Puech, E. "Deux nouveaux sceaux ammonites." RB 83 (1976): 59–62.

965.   ———, and Rofe, A. "L'Inscription de la citadelle d'Amman." RB 80 (1973): 531–46.

965a. Shea, W. H. "The Amman Citadel Inscription Again." PEQ 113 (1981): 103–110.

966. ———. "Milkom as the Architect of Rabbath-Ammon's Natural Defences in the Amman Citadel Inscription." PEQ 111 (1979): 17–25.

967. ———. "The Siran Inscription: Amminadab's Drinking Song." PEQ 110 (1978): 107–12.

968. Thompson, H. and Zayadin, F. "The Tell Siran Inscription." BASOR 212 (1973): 5–11.

969. ———. "The Works of Amminadab." BA 37 (1974): 13–19.

970. Torrey, C. C. "A Few Ancient Seals, I. An Ammonite Seal." AASOR 3 (1923): 103–8.

971. Veenhof, K. R. "De Amman citadel inscriptii." *Phoenix* 18 (1972): 170–79.

972. Yellin-Kallai, Y. "Notes on the New Ammonite Inscription," IEJ 3 (1953): 123–26.

973. Zayadine, F. "Note sur l'inscription de la statue d'Amman J. 1656." *Syria* 51 (1974): 129–36.

974. Zayadine, F., and Thompson, H. "The Ammonite Inscription from Tell Siran." *Berytus* 22 (1973): 115–40.

The Seal and Impression of "ʿAlyah, Maid Servant of Hananʾel." (*Courtesy of the Israel Museum, Jerusalem*)

The Mesha Stele. *(Courtesy of the Musée du Louvre,*
Département des Antiquités Orientales)

6

Moabite Inscriptions

975. Albright, W. F. "Is the Mesha Inscription a Forgery? JQR 35 (1945): 247–50.

976. ———. BASOR 89 (1943): 16, n. 55 (Reading in the Mesha stele).

977. Anderson, F. J. "Moabite Syntax." Or, n.s. 35 (1966): 81–120.

978. Bennett, Wm. H. *The Moabite Stone*. Edinburgh, 1911.

978a. Blau, J. "Short Philological Notes on the Inscription of Meša'." *Maarav* 2 (1980): 143–57.

979. Braslavi, J. "*Kmoshyt*, the Father of Mesha, King of Moab. Zur Neuen Moabitischen Inschrift." BIES 28 (1964): 250–54 (Hebrew).

979a. Drioton, E. "A propos de la stèle du Balou'a." RB 42 (1933): 353–65.

980. Dussaud, R. *Les Monuments palestiniens et judaïques au Musée du Louvre*. Paris, 1912. 4–22.

981. Elitzur, J. "Mesha of Moab and the Mesha Inscription." *Bar-Ilan* 1 (1963): 58–65 (Hebrew).

982. Freedman, D. N. "A Second Mesha Inscription." BASOR 175 (1964): 50–51.

983. Grimme, H. "Ein Schauspiel für Kemosch." ZDMG 66 (1907): 81–85.

984. Horsfield, G., and Vincent, L. H. "Une Stele Égypto-Moabite au Balou'a." RB 41 (1932): 417–44.

985. Lipinski, E. "Etymological and Exegetical Notes on the Mesa Inscription." Or 40 (1971): 325–40.

986. Liver, J. "The Wars of Mesha, King of Moab." PEQ 99 (1967): 14–31.

987. Loewy, A. *Die Echtheit der Moabitischen Inschrift im Louvre aufs Neue Geprüft.* Vienna, 1903.

988. Michaud, H. "Sur un fragment de la stele de Mesa." VT 8 (1958): 302–4.

989. Miller, P. D. "A Note on the Meša Inscription." Or 38 (1969): 461–64.

990. Morag, S. "Meša: A Study of Certain Features of Old Hebrew Dialects." EI 5 (1958): 138–44 (Hebrew).

991. Murphy, R. E. "A Fragment of an Early Moabite Inscription from Dibon." BASOR 125 (1952): 20–23.

992. Nöldeke, T. *Die Inschrift des Königs Mesa von Moab.* Kiel, 1870.

993. Pilcher, E. J. "A Moabite Seal." PEFQS 47 (1915): 42.

994. Puech, E. "Documents épigraphiques de Buseirah." *Levant* 9 (1977): 11–20.

995. Reed, W., and Winnet, F. "A Fragment of an Early Moabite Inscription from Kerak." BASOR 172 (1963): 1–9.

996. Reifenberg, A. "Two Moabite Seals." BIES 12 (1946): 45–47 (Hebrew).

997. Schiffmann, I. "Eine Neue Moabitische Inschrift aus Karcha." ZAW 77 (1965): 324–25.

998. Schlottman, K. *Die Siegessäule Mesa's, Königs der Moabiter.* Halle, 1870.

999. Segert, S. "Die Sprache der Moabitischen Königsinschrift." ArOr 29 (1961): 197–267.

100. Sharpe, S. *An Inquiry into the Age of the Moabite Stone.* London, 1896.

1001. Smend, R. and Socin, A., *Die Inschrift des Königs Mesa von Moab.* Freiburg, 1886.

The Seal and Impression of "Amoṣ the Scribe."
(Courtesy of the Israel Museum, Jerusalem)

1002. Van Zyl, A. H. *The Moabites*. Leiden, 1960.
1003. Winnett, F. "Report of the Director of the School in Jerusalem." BASOR 156 (1959): 4–7.
1004. Yahuda, A. S. "The Story of a Forgery and the Mesha Inscription." JQR 35 (1944): 139–63.

7

Proto-Sinaitic and Proto-Canaanite Inscriptions and the Origins of the Alphabet

1005. Aharoni, Y. "Khirbet Raddana and Its Inscription." IEJ 21 (1972): 130–35.

1006. Albright, W. F. "The Beth-Shemesh Tablet in Alphabetic Cuneiform." BASOR 173 (1964): 51–53.

1007. ———. "The Copper Spatula of Byblus and Proverbs 18:18." BASOR 90 (1943): 35–37.

1008. ———. "The Early Alphabetic Inscriptions from Sinai and Their Decipherment." BASOR 110 (1948): 6–22.

1009. ———. "The Early Evolution of the Hebrew Alphabet." BASOR 63 (1936): 8–12.

1010. ———. "A Hebrew Letter from the Twelfth Century B.C." BASOR 73 (1939): 9–13.

1011. ———. "A Neglected Hebrew Inscription from the Thirteenth Century." AFO 5 (1929): 150–52.

1012. ———. "The Origin of the Alphabet and Ugaritic ABC Again." BASOR 119 (1950): 23–24.

1013. ———. *The Proto-Sinaitic Inscriptions and Their Decipherment*. Cambridge, 1966.

1014. ———. "The So-called Enigmatic Inscription from Byblus." BASOR 116 (1949): 12–14.

1015. ———. "Some Important Recent Discoveries: Alphabetic Origins and the Idrimi Statue." BASOR 118 (1950): 11–20.

1016. ———. "Some Observations on the New Material for the History of the Alphabet." BASOR 134 (1954): 26.

1017. ———. "Some Suggestions for the Decipherment of the Proto-Sinaitic Inscriptions." JPOS 35 (1935): 334–40.

1018. Bange, L. A. *A Study of the Use of Vowel-Letters in Alphabetic Consonantal Writing.* Munich, 1971.

1019. Bauer, H. *Der Ursprung des Alphabets.* Leipzig, 1937.

1020. ———. *Zur Entzifferung der Neuentdeckten Sinaischrift und zur Entstehung des Semitischen Alphabets.* Halle, 1918; reprint ed. Osnabruck, 1966.

1021. Bea, A. "Die Entstehung des Alphabets. *Miscellanea Giovanni Mercati* 6 (1946): 1–35.

1022. Beer, E. F. F. *Inscriptiones Veteres Litteris et Lingua Hucusque Incognitis ad Montem Sinai Magno Numero Servatae quas Pocock, Niebuhr . . . . Explicavit E. F. F. Beer. Fasc. I: Inscriptionum Centuria Litteris Hebraicis Transcripta . . . .* Lipsiae, 1840.

1022a. Beit Arieh, I. "New Discoveries at Serabit el-Khadim." BA 45 (1982): 13–18.

1022b. ———. "New Discoveries in Mine L at Serabit el-Khadem." Qad 14 (1981): 35–7 (Hebrew).

1022c. ———. "New Studies in Mine L at Serabit el-Khadim." EI 15 (1981): 63–8 (Hebrew).

1023. ———; Giveon, R.; and Sass, B. "Explorations at Serabit el-Khadim—1977." TA 5 (1978): 170–87.

1024. Bentley, G. *The Rock Inscriptions in the Peninsula of Sinai; an Inquiry into Their Authorship.* London, 1866.

1025. Bernhardt, K. H. *Die Umwelt des Alten Testaments I, Die Quellen und ihre Erforschung, par. 6, Schriften und Sprachen.* Gutersloh, 1967. 279–362.

1026. Beyer, K. "Die Problematic der Semitischen Konsonantenschrift." *Zeitschrift der Vereinigung der Freunde der Studentenschaft der Universität Heidelburg XIX Jahrgang* 42 (1967): 12–17.

1027. Bissing, F. W., *Die Datierung der Petrieschen Sinaiinschriften.* Munich, 1920.

1028. ———. "Offener Brief an den Herausgeber." OLZ 25 (1922): col. 147–48.

1029. Blackman, A. M. "A New Translation of the Inscription of Hermerre at Serabit." BIFAO 80 (1931): 97–101.

1030. Blake, F. R. "The Development of Symbols for Vowels in the Alphabets Derived from the Phoenician." JAOS 60 (1940): 391–413.

1031. Böhl, F. M. Th. "Die Sichem-Plakette." ZDPV 61 (1938): 1–25.

1032.   Borchardt, L. "Ein Ägyptischen Grab auf der Sinaihalbinsel."
        ZAS 35 (1897): 112–15.

1033.   Bouuaert, J. "Nouvelles hypothèses concernant la constitution
        de l'aphabet proto-sinaitique et des alphabets grecs." *L'Antiquité
        Classique* 14 (1945): 331–51.

1034.   Bowman, R. A. "The Old Aramaic Alphabet at Tell Halaf, the
        Date of the 'Altar' Inscription." AJSL 58 (1941): 359–67.

1035.   Brugsch, H. K. *Wanderung nach den Türkis-minen und der Sinai-
        halbinsel. Mit Drei Tafeln Sinaitischer Inschriften.* Leipzig, 1868.

1036.   Bruston, Ch. "The Serabit Inscriptions." HThR 22 (1929): 175–
        80.

1037.   Buchholz, E. *Schriftgeschichte als Kulturgeschichte.* Bellenhausen,
        1965.

1038.   Burrows, E. "The Tell Duweir Ewer Inscription." PEFQS 66
        (1934): 179–80.

1039.   Butin, R. F. "The Serabit Expedition of 1930. The Protosinaitic
        Inscriptions." HThR 25 (1932): 130–203.

1040.   ———. "Some Egyptian Hieroglyphs of Sinai and Their Rela-
        tionship to the Hieroglyphs of the Proto-Sinaitic Semitic Al-
        phabet." *Mizraim* 2 (1936): 52–56.

1040a. Callaway, J. A. and Cooley, R. E. "A Salvage Excavation at
        Raddana, in Bireh." BASOR 201 (1971): 9–19.

1041.   Cazelles, H. "Deir-Alla et ses tablettes." Sem 15 (1965): 5–21.

1041a. "Nouvelle Écriture sur les tablettes d'argile trouvées à Deir Alla
        (Jordanie)." *Groupe Linguistique d'Études Chamito-Sémitiques* 10
        (1963/66): 66f.

1042.   Cohen, M. *La Grade Invention de l'écriture et son évolution.* 3 vols.
        Paris, 1958.

1043.   Conder, C. R. "Notes by Major Conder, 1. The Sinaitic Inscrip-
        tions." PEFQS (1892), 42–43.

1044.   Cowley, A. E. "The Sinaitic Inscriptions." JEA 15 (1929): 200–
        218.

1045.   ———. *The Sinaitic Inscriptions.* London, 1929 reprint from JEA
        15.

1046.   Cross, F. M. "An Archaic Inscribed Seal from the Valley of
        Aijalon." BASOR 168 (1962): 12–18.

1047.   ———. "The Canaanite Cuneiform Tablet from Taanach."
        BASOR 190 (1968) 41–46.

1048.   ———. "Early Alphabetic Scripts." In F. M. Cross, ed., *Symposia
        Celebrating the Seventy-fifth Anniversary of the Founding of the Ameri-
        can Schools of Oriental Research (1900–1975).* Cambridge, Mass.,
        1979. 97–124.

1049.   ———. "The Evolution of the Proto-Canaanite Alphabet." BASOR 134 (1954): 15–25.

1050.   ———. "Leaves from an Epigraphist's Notebook, #2. The Oldest Phoenician Inscription from the Western Mediterranean." CBQ 36/4 (1974): 490–93.

1050a.   ———. "Newly Found Inscriptions in Old Canaanite and Early Phoenician Scripts." BASOR 238 (1980): 1–20.

1051.   ———. "The Origin and Early Evolution of the Alphabet." EI 8 (1967): 8–24.

1052.   ———. and Freedman, D. N. "An Inscribed Jar Handle from Raddana." BASOR 201 (1971): 19–22.

1053.   ———, and McCarter, P. K. "Two Archaic Inscriptions on Clay Objects from Byblus." *Revista di Studi Fenici* 1 (1973): 3–8.

1054.   ———, and Lambdin, T. O. "A Ugaritic Abecedary and the Origins of the Proto-Canaanite Alphabet." BASOR 160 (1960): 21–26.

1055.   ———, and Milik, J. T. "A Typological Study of the El-Khadr Javelin and Arrow-heads." ADAJ 3 (1956): 15–23.

1056.   Demsky, A. "A Proto-Canaanite Abecedary Dating from the Period of the Judges and Its Implications for the History of the Alphabet." TA 4 (1977): 14–27.

1057.   ———, and Kochavi, M. "An Alphabet from the Days of the Judges." BAR 4/3 (1978): 22–31.

1058.   Dhorme, E. "Appendice au déchiffrement des pseudo-hiéroglyphes de Byblos." *Syria* 27 (1950): 3–4.

1059.   ———.   "Déchiffrement   des   inscriptions   pseudo-hiéroglyphiques de Byblos." *Syria* 25 (1946–48): 1–35.

1060.   ———. "Les Textes pseudo-hiéroglyphiques de Byblos." RA 44 (1950): 193–94.

1061.   Dhorme, P. *Langages et écritures sémitiques.* Paris, 1930.

1062.   Diringer, D. *The Alphabet: A Key to the History of Mankind.* 2 vols. London, 1968.

1063.   ———. "The Alphabet in the History of Civilization." In W. A. Ward, ed., *The Role of the Phoenicians in the Interaction of Mediterranean Civilization.* Beirut, 1968. 33–41.

1063a.   ———. "The Origins of the Alphabet." *Antiquity* 17 (1943): 77–90, 208f.

1064.   ———. "Problems of the Present Day on the Origin of the Phoenician Alphabet." CHM 4 (1957–58): 40–58.

1065.   ———. *The Story of the Aleph Beth.* New York, 1958.

1066.   Doblhofer, E. *Zeichen und Wunder. Die Entzifferung Verschollener Schriften und Sprachen.* Munich, 1964.

1066a.   Donner, H. "Review of W. F. Albright, *The Proto-Sinaitic In-*

scriptions and their Decipherment (Cambridge, 1966)." JSS 12 (1967): 273–81.

1067.   Driver, G. R. *Semitic Writing: From Pictograph to Alphabet*. London, 1970.

1067a. Dunand, M. *Byblia grammata, documents et recherches sur le développement de l'écriture en Phenicie*. Beirut, 1945.

1068.   ———. "Une Nouvelle Inscription énigmatique découverte à Byblos." *Mélanges Maspero* 1 (Cairo, 1935–38): 567–71.

1069.   ———. "Spatule de bronze avec épigraphe phénicienne du XIIIe siècle." BMB 2 (1938): 99–107.

1070.   Dupont-Sommer, A. "L'Inscription phénicienne de la spatule dite d'Asdrubal." ArOr 17/1 (1949): 158–67.

1071.   Dussaud, R. "Nouveau texte phénicien archaïque de Byblos." *Syria* 11 (1930): 306.

1072.   ———. "Review of P. E. Guigues, 'Pointe de flèche en bronze à inscription phénicienne' and S. Ronzevalle, 'Note sur le texte phénicien de la flèche publiée par M. P. E. Guigues'" Syria 8 (1927): 185–6.

1073.   Edzard, D. O., et al. *Kamid el-Loz—Kumidi. Schriftdokumente aus Kamid el-Loz*. Bonn, 1970.

1074.   Eisler, R. "Entdeckung und Entzifferung Kenitischer Inschriften aus dem Anfang des 2. Jahrtausends vor Chr. im Kupferminengebiet der Sinaihalbinsel." BZ (1918–1921), 1–8.

1075.   ———. *"Die Kenitischen Weihinschriften der Hypksoszeit im Berghaugebiet der Sinaihalbinsel, und Einige Andere Unerkannte Alphabet Denkmäler aus der Zeit der XII bis XVIII Dynastie*. Freiburg, 1919.

1076.   Eissfeldt, O. *Von den Anfängen der Phönizischen Epigraphik; nach einem Bisher Unveröffentlichten Brief von Wilhelm Gesenius*. Halle, 1948.

1077.   Euting, J. *Sinaitische Inschriften. Hrsq. Mit. Unterstützung der Königlich Preussischen Akademie der Wissenschaften*. Berlin, 1891.

1078.   Ferron, J. "La Seconde Inscription archaïque de Nora; CIS 145." *Wiener Zeitschrift für die Kunde des Morgenländes* 62 (1969): 62–75.

1079.   Février, J. G. *Histoire de l'écriture*. Paris, 1959.

1080.   ———. "Les Textes de Byblos et la date d'alphabet phénicien." JA 236 (1948): 1–10.

1081.   Flight, J. W. "The Present State of Studies in the History of Writing in the Near East." In E. Grant, ed., *The Haverford Symposium on Archaeology and The Bible*. New Haven, Conn., 1938. 11–135.

1082.   Földes-Papp, K. *Vom Felsbild zum Alphabet. Die Geschichte der*

Schrift von ihren Frühesten Vorstufen bis zur Modernen Lateinischen Schreibschrift. Stuttgart, 1966.

1083.   Forster, C. *The Israelitish Authorship of the Sinaitic Inscriptions Vindicated Against the Incorrect "Observations" in the "Sinai and Palestine" of the Rev. Arthur Penrhyn Stanley . . . A Letter to the Right Honourable the Lord Lyndhurst.* London, 1856.

1084.   ———. *Sinai Photographed; or, Contemporary Records of Israel in the Wilderness.* London, 1862.

1085.   Franken, H. J. "Clay Tablets from Deir Allah, Jordan." VT 14 (1964): 377–79.

1086.   Friedrich, J. "Zur Einleitungsformel der Ältesten Phönizischen Inschriften aus Byblos." *Mélanges Syriens—Dussaud 1* (Paris, 1939): 39–47.

1087.   ———. *Entzifferung Verschollener Schriften und Sprachen.* Berlin, 1966.

1088.   ———. *Geschichte der Schrift. Unter besonderer Berücksichtigung ihrer Geistigen Entwicklung.* Heidelberg, 1966.

1089.   ———. "Die Parallel—Entwicklung der Drei Alten Schrift-Urschopfungen." OrAnt 3 (1959): 95–101.

1090.   Garbini, G. "Considerazioni nell' origine dell' alfabeto." AIUON 16 (1966): 1–18.

1091.   ———. "Gli ostraka di Kamid el-Loz." AIUON 22 (1972): 95–98.

1092.   ———. "Note epigrafiche, C. Le iscrizioni 'proto-cananaiche' del XII e XI secolo a. C." AIUON 34, n.s. 24 (1974): 584–90.

1093.   Gardiner, A. H. "The Egyptian Origin of the Semitic Alphabet." JEA 3 (1916): 1–16.

1094.   ———. "Once Again the Proto-Sinaitic Inscriptions." JEA 48 (1962): 45–48.

1095.   ———. "Origin of Our Alphabet." *Antiquity* 11 (1937): 359–60.

1096.   ———. "The Sinai Script and the Origin of the Alphabet." PEFQS 61 (1929), 48–55.

1097.   ———, and Peet, T. Eric, *The Inscriptions of Sinai.* 2d ed. rev. and augm. by Jaroslav Cerny. London, 1952–1955.

1098.   Gaster, T. H. "The Tell Duweir Ewer Inscription." PEFQS 66 (1934), 176–78.

1099.   Gelb, I. J. *A Study of Writing.* rev. ed. Chicago, 1963.

1100.   ———. *Von der Keilschrift zum Alphabet.* Stuttgart, 1958, translation of I. J. Gelb, *A Study of Writing.* Chicago, 1952.

1101.   Giveon, R. "Two New Hebrew Seals and Their Iconographic Background." PEQ 93 (1961): 38–42.

1102.   Goetze, A. "A Seal Cylinder with an Early Alphabetic Inscription." BASOR 129 (1953): 8–11.

1103. Gordon, C. H. "The Accidental Invention of the Phonemic Alphabet," JNES 29 (1970): 193–97.

1104. Great Britain Ordnance Survey. *Ordnance Survey of the Peninsula of Sinai. Made with the Sanction of the Right Hon. Sir John Pakington, bart., Secretary of State for War, by Captains C. W. Wilson and H. S. Palmer, R. E., Under the Direction of Colonel Sir Henry James . . . Director-General of the Ordnance Survey.* Southampton, 1869.

1105. Greenstein, E. "A Phoenician Inscription in Ugaritic Script?" JANESCU 8 (1976): 49–57.

1106. Grimme, H. *Althebräische Inschriften vom Sinai; Alphabet, Textiliches, Sprachliches mit Folgerungen.* Hanover, 1923.

1107. ———. "Die Altkanaanäische Buchstabenschrift zwischen 1500 und 1250 v. Chr." AFO 10 (1935/1936): 267–81.

1108. ———. *Die Altsinaitischen Buchstaben-Inschriften auf Grund einer Untersuchung der Originale.* Berlin, 1929.

1109. ———. "Die Altsinaitische Felsinschrift Nr. 357." Mus 42 (1929) 33–41.

1110. ———. *Altsinaitische Forschungen. Epigraphisches und Historisches.* Paderborn, 1937.

1111. ———. "Die Buchstabendubletten des Sinai-Alphabetes." *Westfailische Studien* (Leipzig, 1928). 302–12.

1112. ———. "Hjatšepšu und die Sinai-Schriftdenkmäler. Nachwort von K. Sethe." ZDMG 80 (1926): 137–63.

1113. ———. *Die Lösung des Sinaischrift-Problems. Die Altthamudische Schrift.* Münster, 1926.

1114. ———. "Der Name Sinai in den Altsinaitischen Inschriften." Or, n.s. 5 (1936): 88–92.

1115. ———. "Die Neuen Sinaischrift-Denkmäler und ihr Wissenschaftlicher Ertrag." ZDMG 87 (1934): 177–97.

1116. ———. "Südpalästinensische Inschriften in Altsinaitischer Schriftform." Mus 55 (1942): 45–60.

1117. ———. "Zu der Altsinaitischen Inschrift Nr. 363." AFO 12 (1937/38): 59–61.

1118. Guigues, P. E. "Pointe de flèche en bronze à inscription phénicienne," MUSJ 12 (1920): 323–328.

1119. Guy, P. L. O. and Engberg, R. M. *Megiddo Tombs.* Chicago, 1938. 173–76.

1120. Harris, Z. S. *Development of the Canaanite Dialects.* New Haven, Conn., 1939.

1121. Hausmann, U., ed. *Handbuch der Archäologie. Band I: Allgemeine Grundlagen der Archäologie. Begriffe und Methode; Geschichte, Problem der Form, Schriftzeugnisse; Zweiter Teil: Die Schrift und die Schriftzeugnisse.* Munich, 1969. See especially 205–389.

1122. Helck, W. "Zu den Ägyptischen Sinai-Inschriften." OLZ 53 (1958): 421–26.

1123. ———. "Zur Herkunft der Sogenanten 'Phönizischen' Schrift." UF 4 (1972): 41–45.

1124. Hering, E. *Rätsel der Schrift*. Leipzig, 1961.

1125. Hillers, D. R. "An Alphabetic Cuneiform Tablet from Taanach." BASOR 173 (1964): 45–50.

1126. ———. "A Reading in the Beth-Shemesh Tablet." BASOR 199 (1970): 66.

1126a. Hirsch, H. "Tell Deir 'Alla." AFO 21 (1966): 201ff.

1127. Janssens, G. *Contribution au déchiffrement des inscriptions pseudo-hiéroglyphiques de Byblos*. Brussels, 1957.

1128. Jensen, H. *Die Schrift in Vergangenheit und Gegenwart*. Berlin, 1958. Eng. trans., *Sign, Symbol and Script*, London, 1970.

1129. Jirku, A. "Entzifferung der Gublitischen Schrift durch E. Dhorme." FuF 26 (1950): 90–92.

1130. ———. "Zum Ursprung des Alphabets." ZDMG 100/2 (1950): 201–14.

1131. Jomier, J. "Les Graffiti 'sinaïtiques' du Wadi Abou Daradj." RB 61 (1954): 419–24.

1132. Kallner, R. B. "Two Inscribed Sherds from Tell es-Sarem." Kedem 2 (1945): 11–13 (Hebrew).

1133. Kochavi, M. "An Ostracon of the Period of the Judges from 'Izbet Sarṭah." TA 4 (1977): 1–13.

1134. ———, and Demsky, A. "A Proto-Canaanite Abecedary from 'Izbet Sarṭa." Qad 11 (1978): 61–67 (Hebrew).

1135. Lake, K., and Blake, R. "The Serabit Inscriptions. The Rediscovery of the Inscriptions." along with "The Decipherment and Significance of the Inscriptions," by Romain F. Butin. HThR 21 (1928): 1–67.

1136. Lake, K.; Blake, R.; and Johnson, A. W. "The Serabit Inscriptions." ASAE 27 (1927): 238–40.

1137. Landgraf, J. "The Manahat Inscription: *LŠDḤ*." *Levant* 3 (1971): 92–95.

1138. Lapp, P. W. "The 1966 Excavations at Tell Ta'annak." BASOR 185 (1967): 2–39.

1139. Leibovitch, J. "The Date of the Proto-Sinaitic Inscriptions. Additional Note by W. F. Albright." Mus 76 (1963): 201–5.

1140. ———. "Deux Nouvelles Inscriptions Protosinaïtiques." Mus 74 (1961): 461–466.

1141. ———. *Les Inscriptions protosinaïtiques*. Cairo, 1934.

1142. ———. "Die Petrieschen Sinai-Schrift-Denkmäler." ZDMG 84 (1930): 1–14.

Ostracon from Izbet Sarteh. *(Courtesy of the Institute of Archaeology, Tel Aviv University.)* Moshe Weinberg photo.

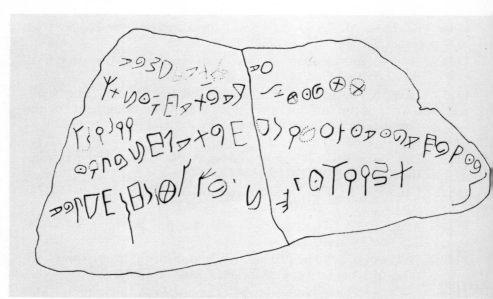

Drawing of the Ostracon from Izbet Sarteh. *(Courtesy of the Institute of Archaeology, Tel Aviv University)*

1143. ———. "Le Tesson de Tell Nagila (inscription protocananéenne)." Mus 78 (1965): 229–30.

1144. Lemaire, A. "Une Novelle Inscription paléo-hébraïque sur carafe." RB 83 (1976): 55–58.

1145. Lenormant, Ch. F. *Essai sur la propagation de l'alphabet phénicien dans l'ancien monde.* Paris, 1874–75.

1146. ———. *Sur l'origine Chrétienne des inscriptions sinaïtiques.* Paris, 1859. Extrait no. 1 de l'année 1859 du *Journal Asiatique.* Tiré à cent exemplaires. no. 94).

1146a. Levine, B. A. "The Deir 'Allā Plaster Inscriptions." JAOS 101 (1981): 195–205.

1146b. Luria, B. Z. "Whose Paleo-Hebrew Script?" *Beth Mikra* 26 (1980): 98–101 (Hebrew).

1147. Maag, V. "Die Schrift." In H. Schmökel, ed., *Kulturgeschichte des Alten Orient III, VIII.* Stuttgart, 1961. 519–44.

1148. Maisler, B. "Zur Urgeschichte des Phoenizisch-Hebraeischen Alphabets." JPOS 18 (1938): 278–91.

1149. Mansfeld, G. "Deux 'Ostrakons' incisés à écriture paléo-canaanéenne du Tell de Kamid el-Lōz." BMB 22 (1969): 67–75.

1150. Martin, M. F. "A Preliminary Report after Reexamination of the Byblian Inscriptions." Or 30 (1961): 46–78.

1151. ———. "Revision and Reclassification of the Proto-Byblian Signs." Or 31 (1962): 250–71, 339–83.

1152. ———. "A Twelfth Century Bronze Palimpsest." RSO 37 (1962): 175–93.

1153. May, H. G. "Moses and the Sinai Inscriptions." BA 8 (1945): 93–99.

1154. McCarter, P. K. *The Antiquity of the Greek Alphabet and the Early Phoenician Scripts.* Missoula, Mont., 1975.

1155. ———. "The Early Diffusion of the Alphabet." BA 37 (1974): 62–66.

1156. ———, and Coote, R. B. "The Spatula from Byblos." BASOR 212 (1973): 16–22.

1157. Mendenhall, G. E. "A New Chapter in the History of the Alphabet." BMB 24 (1971): 13–18.

1158. Meshel, Z. "Kuntilat 'Ajrud, 1975–1976." IEJ 27 (1977): 52–53.

1159. Mesnil du Buisson, C. "Le Cylindre Sceau archaïque de Byblos réexaminé," *Berytus* 24 (1975–76): 89–119.

1160. Milik, J. T. "Fléches à inscriptions phéniciennes au Musée National Libanais." BMB 16 (1961): 1–3, 108.

1161. ———, and Cross, F. M. "Inscribed Javelin-Heads from the Period of the Judges: a Recent Discovery in Palestine." BASOR 134 (1954): 5–15.

1162. Moriarty, F. L. "Early Evidence of Alphabetic Writing." CBQ 2 (1951): 135–45.

1163. Moritz, B. *Der Sinaikult in Heidnischer Zeit.* Berlin, 1916.

1164. Mountford, J. "Writing." *Encyclopedia of Linguistics, Information and Control.* Oxford, 1969.

1165. Naveh, J. "Some Considerations on the Ostracon from 'Izbet Sarṭah." IEJ 28 (1978): 31–35.

1166. Naville, E. *L'Évolution de la langue égyptienne et les langues sémitiques.* Paris, 1920.

1167. Obermann, J. "An Early Phoenician Political Document with a Parallel to Judges 11:24." JBL 58 (1939): 229–42.

1169. Petrie, W. M. F. *Ancient Gaza II.* London, 1932. Pl. 40.

1170. ———. "The Alphabet in the Twelfth Dynasty." *Ancient Egypt* 6 (1921): 1–3.

1171. ———. *Researches in Sinai.* London, 1906.

1172. Pilcher, E. J. "The Origin of the Alphabet." PSBA 26 (1904): 168ff.

1173. Pritchard, J. B. *Sarepta: A Preliminary Report on the Iron Age.* Philadelphia, University Museum, 1975. 101.

1174. Rainey, A. F. "Notes on Some Proto-Sinaitic Inscriptions." IEJ 25 (1975): 106–116.

1174a. ———. "Some Minor Points in Two Proto-Sinaitic Inscriptions." IEJ 31 (1981): 92–94.

1175. Röllig, W. "Die Alphabetschrift." In U. Hausmann, ed., *Handbuch der Archäologie, I, Allgemeine Grundlagen der Archäologie.* Munich, 1969. Zweiter Teil: *Die Schrift und die Schriftzeugnisse,* erster abschnitt, erster kap., F. 289–302.

1176. ———, and Mansfeld, G. "Zwei Ostraka von Tell Kamid-el-Loz und ein Neuer Aspekt für die Entstehung des Kanaanäischen Alphabets." WO 5 (1970): 253–70.

1177. Ronzevalle, S. "Note sur le texte phénicien de la flèche publiée par M. P. E. Guiges." MUSJ 11 (1926): 325–58.

1178. Sauer, G. "Die Tafeln von Deir Alla." ZAW 81 (1969): 145–56.

1179. Schaumberger, J. B. "Die Angeblichen Mosaischen Inschriften vom Sinai." Bib 5 (1925), 26–49, 156–64, 465.

1180. Schmandt-Besserat, D. "Reckoning Before Writing." Arch 32 (1979): 22–31.

1181. Schmokel, H. "Zur Vorgeschichte des Alphabets." FuF 26 (1950): 153–55.

1182. Schneider, H. "Die Neuentdeckte Sinaischrift." OLZ 24 (1921): cols. 241–46.

1183. Seger, J. D. "The Lahav Research Project in Israel." Arch 32 (1979): 50–52.

1184. Sethe, K. H. "Die Neuentdeckte Sinai-Schrift und die Ent-stehung der Semitischen Schrift." In *Nachrichten von der K. Gesellschaft der Wissenschaften zu Göttingen* (Philos.-hist. Klasse, 1917). 437–475.

1185. ———. "Die Petrieschen Sinaifund. Vortrag Gehalten in der Vorderasiatisch-Ägyptischen Gesellschaft am 8. Dezember 1925. . . ." FuF (1926), 2f.

1186. ———. "Der Ursprung des Alphabets." In *Nachrichten von der K. Gesellschaft der Wissenschaften zu Göttingen* (Philos.-hist. Klasse, 1916). 87–161.

1189. ———. *Vom Bilde zum Buchstaben. Die Entstehungsgeschichte der Schrift.* Leipzig, 1939.

1190. ———. "Die Wissenschaftliche Bedeutung der Petrieschen Sinaifunde und die Angeblichen Moseszeugnisse." ZDMG 80 (1926): 24–54.

1191. Sharpe, S. *Hebrew Inscriptions from the Valleys Between Egypt and Mount Sinai in their Original Characters, with Translations and an Alphabet.* London, 1875–1876.

1192. Shea, W. H. "The Byblos Spatula Inscription." JAOS 97 (1977): 164–70.

1193. ———. "The Inscribed Late Bronze Jar Handle from Tell Halif." BASOR 232 (1978): 78–80.

1194. Siegel, J. L. "The Date and the Historical Background of the Sinaitic Inscriptions." AJSL 49 (1932–33): 46–52.

1195. Sobelman, H. "The Proto-Byblian Inscriptions: A Fresh Approach." JSS 6 (1961): 226–45.

1196. Speiser, E. A. "A Note on Alphabetic Origins." BASOR 121 (1951): 17–21.

1197. Sprengling, M. *The Alphabet, its Rise and Development from the Sinai Inscriptions.* Chicago, 1931.

1198. Stager, L. E. "An Inscribed Potsherd from the Eleventh Century." BASOR 194 (1969): 45–52.

1199. Starkey, J. L. "Palestine Clues to the Origin of the Alphabet." ILN Nov. 27, 1937. 968.

1200. Starr, R. F. S., and Butin, R. F. *Excavations and Proto-Sinaitic Inscriptions at Serabit el Khadem. Report of the Expedition of 1935.* London, 1936.

1201. Stieglitz, R. R. "The Ugaritic Cuneiform and the Canaanite Linear Scripts." JNES 30 (1971): 135–39.

1202. Stube, R. "Die Sinai-Inschriften: Neue Beiträge zum Ursprung des Alphabets." *Deutscher Verein für Buchwesen und Schrifttum. Zeitschrift* 1 (1918): 97–100.

1203. Sukenik, E. L. "Note on the Sherd from Tell es-Sarem." Kedem 2 (1945): 15 (Hebrew).

1204. Sznycer, M. "Quelques Remarques à propos de la formation de l'alphabet phénicien." Sem 24 (1974): 5–12.

1205. Taylor, I. *The Alphabet: An Account of the Origin and Development of Letters.* rev. ed., 2 vols. New York, 1899.

1206. Teixidor, J. "An Archaic Inscription from Byblos." BASOR 225 (1977): 70–71.

1207. Torczyner, H. "The Canaanite Inscriptions *l'zrb'l* from Gebal." *Leshonenu* 14 (1946): 158–65 (Hebrew).

1208. ———. "The Origin of the Alphabet." JQR 41 (1950): 83–109, 159–97, 277–301.

1209. Tschichold, J. *Geschichte der Schrift in Bildern.* Basel, 1940.

1210. Tuch, Dr. "Ein und Zwanzig Sinaitische Inschriften. Versuch Einer Erklarung." ZDMG 3 (1849): 129–215.

1211. ———. "Ueber Eine Sinaitische Inschrift." ZDMG 2 (1848): 395–97.

1212. Van den Branden, A. "Anciennes Inscriptions sémitiques." BibOr 17 (1960): 218–22.

1213. ———. "Le Déchiffrement des inscriptions protosinaïtiques," *al-Machriq* 52 (1958): 361–95.

1213a. ———. "Comment lire les textes de Deir 'Alla?" VT 15 (1965): 129–49, 532–35.

1214. ———. "Les Inscriptions de Tell Deir 'Alla." *al-Machriq* 61 (1967): 357–70.

1214a. ———. "L'Inscription en caractères protosinaïtiques sur le cylindre de M. Grossman." *Melto* 4 (1968): 112–23.

1215. ———. "L'Inscription en caractères protosinaïtiques sur le prisme de Lakish." *Melto* 3 (1967): 135–45.

1216. ———. "Les Inscriptions protosinaïtiques." OrAnt 1 (1962): 197–214.

1216a. ———. "Nuove iscrizioni protosinaitiche." BeO 23 (1981): 213–20.

1217. ———. "L'Origine des alphabets protosinaïtiques, arabes préislamiques et phéniciens." BibOr 19 (1962): 198–206.

1218. ———. "Qui sont les auteurs des inscriptions protosinaïtiques?" *Melto* 2 (1966): 273–89.

1219. ———. "Steine die Sprechen (holl)." TH Land 11 (1958): 97–103.

1220. ———. "Le Tesson de Tell Nagila." *Melto* 2 (1966): 131–37.

1221. Volter, D. *Die Althebräischen Inschriften vom Sinai und ihre Historische Bedeutung.* Leipzig, 1924.

1222. Weill, R. *Recueil des inscriptions égyptiennes du Sinai, bibliographie, texte, traduction et commentaire, précédé de la géographie, de l'histoire et de la bibliographie des établissements égyptiens de la péninsule.* Paris, 1904.

1223.   Weule, K. *Vom Kerbstock zum Alphabet. Urformen der Schrift.* Stuttgart, 1928.

1224.   Windfuhr, G. L. "The Cuneiform Signs of Ugarit." JNES 29 (1970): 48–51.

1225.   Yadin, Y. *Hazor I.* Jerusalem, 1958. 99, 160.

1226.   ———. "Note on a Proto-Canaanite Inscription from Lachish." PEQ 91 (1959): 130–31.

1227.   Yeivin, S. *The History of the Jewish Script, I.* Jerusalem, 1939. (Hebrew).

1228.   ———. "A New Ugaritic Inscription from Palestine." *Kedem* 2 (1945): 32–41.

1229.   ———. "The Palestino-Sinaitic Inscriptions." PEQ 69 (1937): 180–93.

1230.   ———. "Miscellanea Epigraphica I–IV." *Bulletin of the Museum Ha-aretz* 14 (1972): 79–83.

1230a.   ———. Note sur une pointe de flèche inscrite provenant de la Beqaa (Liban). RB, n.s. 65 (1958): 585–88.

1231.   ———. "Sinaitic Inscriptions in Israelite Territory." BIES 5 (1941): 1–9 (Hebrew).

1232.   Zolli, E. *Ideogenesi e morfologia dell'antico sinaitico, un contributo alla storia del divenire dell'alfabeto graeco-romano.* Trieste, 1925.

1233.   ———. *Un iscrizione votiva antico-sinaitica.* . . . Rome, 1926. Extract from *Studi e materiali di storia delle religioni* 2 (1926).

1234.   ———. *Il nome della lettera "cadde", il nome divino Shaddaj.* Florence, 1926.

1235.   ———. *Sinaischrift und Griechisch-lateinisches Alphabet, Ursprung und Ideologie.* Trieste, 1925.

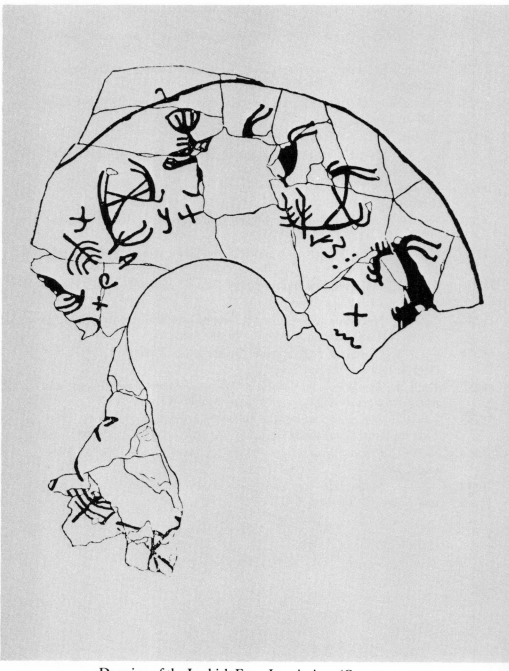

Drawing of the Lachish Ewer Inscription. *(Courtesy of the Israel Museum, Jerusalem)*

PART II
Indexes

Chronological Index of Inscriptions

Date	Site	Artifact	Bibliographic Reference Number
1850-1500	Serabit el-Khadim	steliform inscriptions	1008, 1013, 1017, 1019, 1020, 1022-1024, 1027, 1029, 1032, 1033, 1035, 1036, 1039, 1040, 1043-1045, 1066a, 1074, 1075, 1077, 1083, 1084, 1093-1097, 1104, 1106-1115, 1122, 1131, 1135, 1136, 1139-1142, 1146, 1153, 1163, 1170, 1171, 1174, 1174a, 1177, 1179, 1182, 1184, 1185, 1190, 1191, 1194, 1197, 1200, 1202, 1210, 1211, 1213, 1214, 1216-1218, 1221, 1222, 1231-1235.
1800-1600	Gezer	fragment of a cult stand	26, 119, 180, 181, 565, 1013, 1063a, 1067.
2100-1500	Byblos	spatulas, tablets	1007, 1058-1060, 1067, 1067a, 1069-1071, 1080, 1086, 1127, 1150, 1151, 1156, 1159, 1192, 1195, 1206, 1207.
1800-1400	Shechem	incantation plaque	26, 419, 1013, 1031, 1063a, 1067.
1800-1650 (1300-1100?)	Tell es-Sarem	plaque	26, 587, 588, 1063a, 1067, 1132, 1203.
1700-1550	Lachish	dagger	26, 299, 305, 322, 330, 1013, 1063a, 1067, 1229, 1231.
1600-1400	Tell Nagila	ostracon	1143, 1220.
1550-1200	Lahav	jar handle	1183.
1500-1400	Byblos	ostracon	1067, 1067a.
1500-1200	Tell Halif	jar handle	1193.
1450-1400	Lachish	prism	26, 299, 322, 1013, 1063a, 1215, 1229, 1231.
1450-1300	Lachish	censor lid	26, 299, 322, 1063a, 1067, 1229, 1231.

Chronological Index of Inscriptions

Date	Site	Artifact	Bibliographic Reference Number
1400–1200	Lachish	bowl #1	299, 322, 330, 1013, 1049, 1067, 1229, 1231.
1400–1300	Tell el-Hesi	octracon	26, 563-565, 1039, 1040, 1063a.
1400–1300	?	seal ("St. Louis seal" or "Goetze seal")	1013, 1046, 1049, 1051, 1102, 1214a.
1400–1300	Tell et-Taʿajjul	ostracon	26, 1049, 1051, 1063a, 1067, 1169.
1400–1200	Byblos	fragmentary stone ("enigmatic inscription")	1013, 1014, 1049, 1067a, 1068, 1107.
1400–1200	Mount Tabor	knife	1228.
1400–1100	Beth Shemesh	ostracon	25, 105, 106a, 108, 1013, 1051, 1063a, 1067, 1106, 1126.
1400–1100	Beth Shemesh	tablet (Ugaritic)	110, 1006.
1350–1250	Hazor	ostracon ("dipinto")	1225.
1350–1200	Megiddo	gold ring	26, 332, 1013, 1063a, 1067, 1119.
1350–1150	Byblos	clay objects ("A" and "B")	1053, 1206.
1300–1200	Taanach	tablet (Ugaritic)	1047, 1125, 1138.

114

Chronological Index of Inscriptions

Date	Site	Artifact	Bibliographic Reference Number
1300-1100	Tell el-Ḥesi	fragment of plate	24, 562-565, 1011, 1067.
1300-1200	Lachish	ewer	26, 268, 299, 322, 323, 1013, 1038, 1049, 1063a, 1067, 1098, 1116, 1161, 1215, 1226, 1229, 1231.
1200-1100	Izbet Sarṭah	abecedary tablet	889a, 903a, 1050a, 1056, 1057, 1133, 1134, 1165.
1200-1100	el-Khadr, Biqaʿ, Ruweiseh	arrowheads	26, 1013, 1016, 1050a, 1055, 1063a, 1067, 1067a, 1072, 1118, 1152, 1160, 1161, 1177, 1230a.
1200-1100	Byblos	spatula	1010, 1067, 1067a, 1167, 1207, 1230a.
1200-1100	Revadim (Aijalon Valley)	seal	718, 737, 788, 856, 1013, 1046, 1101, see Seal Index.
1200-1100	Baluʿah	stele	979a, 984.
1200-900	Tell Deir Allah	tablets	910c, 934a, 1041, 1041a, 1085, 1126a, 1146a, 1178, 1213a.
1200-1000	Khirbet Raddana	jar handle	1005, 1040a, 1052, 1230.
1200-1000	Qubur el-Walaydah	bowl	1050a.
1200-1000	Manahat	ostracon	1137, 1198.
1200-1000	Kamid el-Loz	ostraca	1073, 1091, 1149, 1176.
1100-1000	Nora	fragment	1050, 1078.
1100-1000	Sarepta	ewer	1105, 1173.
1100-1000	Tell Jemmeh	ostracon	24, 732, 791a.

115

Chronological Index of Inscriptions

Date	Site	Artifact	Bibliographic Reference Number
1100-800	Kuntilat ʿAjrud	a. stone bowl b. abecedary	903a, 911-913a, 1158. 903a, 911-913a, 1158.
1000-900	Gezer	calendar	7, 24, 27, 28, 35, 41a(v. 3, p. 36-42, 189f, 279), 46, 50, 60a, 61(v. 3, n. 1201), 67a, 68a, 118, 119, 121-125, 128, 133-136, 139a, 141-145, 147-151, 154, 155, 157-159, 167, 169, 173-178, 183-185, 188-190, 368, 374, 978 (appendix 2), 1148.
1000-900	Shiqmona	storage jar, bronze disc	424, 425, 425a.
1000-900	Tell en-Nasbeh	ostracon	50, 580, 583-586.
900-800(?)	Tell Beit Mirsim	ostracon	555-560.
900-700	Kuntilat ʿAjrud	ostraca	873a, 883a, 884b, 890a, 911-913a, 1158.
875-825	Amman	citadel inscription	936-938, 945, 949, 951, 952, 954, 957, 960, 965-966, 971, 972, 973.
850-750	Samaria	ivories	50, 359, 409.
850-750	Samaria	1910 ostraca	6, 24, 27, 33, 35, 46, 56, 60a, 68a, 344-349, 357-360, 362-366, 368-400, 403-406, 410, 414-418, 622, 624.
850-725	Samaria	ostracon C1101	24, 27, 35, 46, 50, 60a, 346, 369, 404, 602.
850-750	Tell el-Hesi	ostracon	24, 42, 61(v. 3, p. 1241), 562a, 563, 564, 693, 714.
850-800	el-Kerak	fragmentary stele	35, 979, 982, 995, 997.

Chronological Index of Inscriptions

Date	Site	Artifact	Bibliographic Reference Number
850-800	Dibon	Mesha stele	13, 27, 33, 35, 42, 46, 60a, 68a, 975-981, 983, 985-990, 992, 998-1002, 1004.
850-700	Hazor	a. storage jars	35, 46, 198, 199.
		b. ostracon	197a, 200.
800-700	Arad	bowl	73.
800-700	Samaria	ostracon	24, 406.
800-700	Beer-sheba	a. storage jar	102.
		b. bowl	102.
		c. ostracon	102.
800-700	Dan	ostracon	113, 114.
800-700	Beth-Shemesh	ostracon	24, 111.
800-700	Khirbet el-Kom	tombs	254-256, 258-258b, 873a.
800-700	Jerusalem	ivory	222a.
800-700	Samaria	stele	50, 360, 408, 1227.
800-700	Siloam	tunnel	6, 9, 13, 14, 24, 27, 28, 33, 35, 35a, 41, 41a(v. 1, p. 53, 310; v. 2, p. 71, 190), 42, 43a, 45, 46, 50, 60a, 64, 65, 70a, 71, 133, 138, 169, 363, 426-544, 660, 775, 877a, 884a, 978, 980, 1166, 1172.
800-700	Tell Qasile	ostraca	35, 46, 50, 589-591, 902, 921.
800-600	Kadesh-Barnea	ostracon	886a, 906a.
800-600	Jerusalem	ostracon	213a, 229a.
750-650	Megiddo	storage jar	50, 333, 334.

117

Chronological Index of Inscriptions

Date	Site	Artifact	Bibliographic Reference Number
750-700	Jerusalem	stone fragment	240, 241.
750-700	Nimrud	ostracon	961a.
750-650	Siloam Village	tombs	9, 24, 27, 35, 42, 46, 50, 70a, 449, 545-554, 807.
750-650	Jerusalem	storage jar	221a.
750-650	Khirbet el-Kom	storage jar	256.
750-650	Hebron area	storage jar	875.
700-600	Tell el-Ful	jar handles	561.
700-600	Jerusalem	Ophel ostracon	2, 24, 27, 35, 50, 206, 207, 217, 243, 245, 246, 247a, 248.
700-600	Jerusalem	stone fragment	229a.
650-600	Yavne Yam	a. ostracon - letter	27, 35, 599-619.
		b. ostracon	609.
650-600	Heshbon	ostraca	944.
650-600	Lachish	jar handles	35, 273, 291a, 330, 843.
650-587	Arad	ostraca	35, 73-81, 83-95, 622.
650-550	Azor	burial jar	99, 100.
650-587	Gibeon	jar handles	35, 191-197.
650-587	Tell el-Kheleifeh	ostraca	566-579.
650-600	Lachish	wine decanter	271a.

118

Chronological Index of Inscriptions

Date	Site	Artifact	Bibliographic Reference Number
650-550	Dibon	fragmentary stele	991.
650-500	Khirbet Beit Lei	tomb inscriptions	35, 250-253.
600-587	Lachish	ostraca	27, 33, 35, 45, 46, 60a, 68a, 260-267, 270, 270a, 272, 273, 276-287, 292-301, 304-306, 308-317, 319-321, 328-330.
600-550	Jerusalem	storage jar	875.
600-550	Tell Siran	bottle	941a, 941b, 943b, 947, 956a, 961, 967-969, 974.
500-400	Ashdod	ostracon	98.
450-350	Tell el-Kheleifeh	ostraca	566-579.
450-400	Bat Yam	storage jar	101.
450-350	Elephantine	ostracon	115, 116, 932.
400-300	Shiqmona	a. abecedary ostracon	424, 425.
		b. storage jars	424, 425.
300-200	Khirbet el-Kom	ostraca	257, 257a, 259.
200-0	Jerusalem	tombs	212, 213, 223, 230, 249.
200-0	Jerusalem	a. monumental inscription	224, 226, 227, 249.
200-0	Herodium	b. stone bowl abecedary	226a. 921b.

Chronological Index of Inscriptions

Date	Site	Artifact	Bibliographic Reference Number
0-400	Beth Shearim	tombs	104.

Development of the Alphabet

The following Bibliographic Reference Numbers treat the development of alphabetic writing by surveying, in varying degrees, the corpus of inscriptional material.

26, 1009, 1012, 1015, 1016, 1018, 1019, 1021, 1025, 1026, 1028, 1030, 1033, 1034, 1037, 1042, 1048, 1049, 1051, 1054, 1061-1067, 1076, 1079, 1081, 1082, 1087-1090, 1099, 1100, 1103, 1120, 1121, 1123, 1124, 1128-1130, 1145, 1147, 1148, 1154, 1157, 1162, 1164, 1166, 1172, 1175, 1180, 1181, 1186, 1189, 1196, 1197, 1201, 1204, 1205, 1209, 1212, 1223, 1227.

Index of Hebrew Personal Seals
(according to site)

Site	Artifact	"seal of..."	Date	Bibliographic Reference Number
Arad	seal	dršyhw	800-700	73(#109), 76, 620, 749(#86), 856(#212), 857(#212).
Arad	seal	brkyhw	675-625	36a(#130), 73(#108), 82, 748(H8), 749(#54), 856(#230).
Arad	seals	ʾlyšb	625-600	36a(#58), 73(#106), 82, 748(H5), 749(#11), 856(#231), 857(#231).
Arad	seal	ʾlyšb	625-600	36a(#57), 73(#105), 82, 748(H6), 749(#12), 856(#231).
Arad	seal	ʾlyšb	625-600	36a(#58), 73(#107), 82, 748(H7), 749(#13), 856(#232).
Aijalon Valley (Revadim)	seal	ʾbʾ	1200-1100	718, 737, 788, 1013, 1046, 1101, 856(#204).
Ascalon	seal	rmʿ	700-650	24(#14), 61(v.3, p.1274), 170, 694, 733(#4), 748(H62), 847, 856(#14).
Ascalon	seal	ʾbgyl	?	24(#62), 35, 41(s, p.11), 41a(v.1, p.56), 42(p.504), 61(v.1, p.383), 648(v.1, p.22), 701, 714, 856(#62), 857(#62).
Ashdod	seal	šlmʾl	550-500	50(p.60), 748(Ar26), 810.
Azor	seal	ʾdtʾ	650-600	36(#134), 50(p.62-63), 623, 648(v.3, p.80), 748(H36), 749(#32), 805(p.38), 810, 856(#152).

*Major collections of seals may be found under Bibliographic Reference Numbers: 8, 10, 13, 15a, 24, 36a, 50, 646, 648-653, 676-678, 681a, 702-708, 719, 722, 733, 747a-749, 766a, 771, 785, 793, 799, 805, 806, 808, 810-812, 816, 816a, 819, 853, 856, 857.

121

Index of Hebrew Personal Seals
(according to site)

Site	Artifact	"seal of..."	Date	Bibliographic Reference Number
Beth Shemesh	impression	ḥsdʾ	775-725	50(p.74), 107(v.5, p.80), 748(H45), 749(#25).
Beth Shemesh	impression	bky	750-650	107(v.5, p.82-83), 112, 748(H38), 749(#16).
Beth Shemesh	impression	sdq	750-700	50(p.75), 107(v.5, p.83), 748(H58).
Beth Shemesh	impression	tnḥm	750-700	50(p.75), 107(v.5, p.83-84), 748(H158).
Beth Shemesh	impression	ʾlyqm	725-700	36a(#22,23), 107(v.5, p.80), 557-560, 626, 648(v.1, p.351), 713, 748(H31), 749(#9), 781, 852(v.2, p.813), 856(#108), 857(#108), 866; see also Ramat Raḥel, Tell Beit Mirsim for other occurrences of this impression.
Beth Shemesh	impression	ksʾ	725-700	50(p.75), 107(v.5, p.84), 648(v.2, p.920), 748(H50), 856(#107), 857(#107).
Beth Shemesh	impression	mnḥm	725-675	50(p.74), 107(v.5, p.81-82), 748(H52).
Beth Shemesh	seal	ḥʾh	700-675	24(#48), 109, 748(H40), 856(#48).
Beth Shemesh	impression	spn	700-675	50(p.74), 107(v.5, p.80-81), 748(H59).
Beth Shemesh	seal	ʿdyhw	675-625	50(p.63), 107(v.5, p.81), 748(H55), 749(#58), 856(#154).
Beth-Zur	impression	gʾlyhw	625-575	36a(#21), 68a(p.223), 648(v.2, p.160), 748(H39), 749(#7), 805, 831, 832, 856(#110), 857(#110).
Dan	seal	ʿzʾ	900-750	718, 737, 788, 856(#205).

Index of Hebrew Personal Seals
(according to site)

Site	Artifact	"seal of..."	Date	Bibliographic Reference Number
Deir Aben?	seal	mꜤsyhw	800-600	41(f.p.11), 41a(v.2, p.70), 696, 707, 708, 714, 861.
En Gedi	seal	mtnyhw	650-600	782, 910a(pl.26).
En Gedi	seal	nmrtʾ(?)	650-500	781a, 788, 856(#208).
En Gedi	seal	ʾryhw	625-600	748(H27), 781a, 782, 788, 856(#207), 857(#207), 910a(pl.26).
En Gedi	seal	ṭbšlm	600-500	36a(#136), 748(H28).
En Gedi	impression	nrʾ(?)	600-575	748(H29), 782, 910a(pl.26).
Gaza	seal	ytn(?)	625-575	50(p.64), 748(P7), 749(#128), 812, 856(#158), 857(#158).
Gezer	seal	ʾlyhw	675-625	739, 748(H154).
Gezer	seal	šbnyhw	650-600	24(#15), 50(p.67), 170, 733(#77), 748(H64), 847, 856(#15).
Gezer	impression	bnr	700-600(?)	41a(v.2, p.146), 50(#82), 61(v.3, p.1247), 120, 128, 158(p.225), 162, 652a.
Gezer	seal	h	700-600(?)	24(#79), 158(p.295), 856(#79).
Gibeon	impression	nhm	700-600	195(p.27), 856(#186).
Gibeon	impression	tnhm	700-600	195(p.28), 856(#187).

Index of Hebrew Personal Seals
(according to site)

Site	Artifact	"seal of..."	Date	Bibliographic Reference Number
Gibeon	impression	ʿzryhw	700-600	195(p.28), 856(#188).
Gibeon	impressions	mšlm(?)	700-600	195(p.28), 856(#189-190).
Gibeon	impression	nn(?)	700-600	195(p.28), 856(#191).
Gibeon	impression	tnḥm	650-600	195(p.29), 856(#192); see also Lachish, Ramat Rahel for other occurrences of this impression
Hebron area	impression	yhwzrḥ	725-675	228a(p.179), 748(H3), 749(#4), 751.
Hebron(?)	seal	mʿsyhw	725-700	749(H115), 839(pl.63), 872.
Horvat Shovav	impression	bky	700-600	802.
Jericho	impressions	sgnd/hgr/yhwd	500-350	201, 203-205, 638, 719, 856(#184).
Jerusalem (Mt. Zion)	seal	qnyw	775-725	24(#13), 42(p.486,504), 50(p.66), 61(v.1, p.327), 698, 714, 733(#74), 748(H60), 856(#13), 857(#13).
Jerusalem?	seal	šlm	750-600	796.
Jerusalem area	seal	šlm	725-675	50(p.60), 748(H136), 812, 856(#147), 857(#147).
Jerusalem	seal	ḥgy	725-675	24(#20), 41(p.11), 42(p.270), 648(v.3, p.82), 682, 708b, 714, 748(H150), 771(p.45), 856(#20).

Index of Hebrew Personal Seals
(according to site)

Site	Artifact	"seal of..."	Date	Bibliographic Reference Number
Jerusalem (Jewish Quarter)	impression	ṣpn	725-600	630.
Jerusalem (Ophel)	seal	yšmꜥʾl	700-675	24(#45?), 41(i, p.11), 215, 216, 231, 235, 236, 683, 714, 748(H48), 795, 856(#45?).
Jerusalem	impression	hwšꜥm	700-675	748(H88), 783(p.181).
Jerusalem	seal	ḥmyʾhl	700-600	721, 749(#34).
Jerusalem (Jewish Quarter)	impression	mnḥm	700-600	630.
Jerusalem (SW Temple Mount)	impression	hwšꜥm	700-600(?)	224, 783(p.181).
Jerusalem	seal	šbnyhw	700-600	24(p.179).
Jerusalem?	seal	mꜥdnh	700-600	637, 738b, 863a, 872a.
Jerusalem (Solomon's Pools)	seal	ḥnnyhw	675-625	24(#50), 648(v.5, p.928), 748(H44), 749(#64), 795, 856(#50).
Jerusalem (Citadel)	seal	mtnyhw	675-625	36a(#133), 208, 209, 227, 748(H54), 749(#66), 857(#268).

Index of Hebrew Personal Seals
(according to site)

Site	Artifact	"seal of..."	Date	Bibliographic Reference Number
Jerusalem	seal	dmlyhw	675-625	24(#19), 42(p.326, 369), 61(v.3, p.1273), 648(v.3, p.80), 694, 712, 714, 748(H151), 818, 847, 856(#19), 857(#19).
Jerusalem (Ophel)	seal	ḥgy	675-625	233, 748(H41), 788, 856(#213).
Jerusalem area	seal	rbyhw	625-600	50(p.65), 748(H61), 749(#67), 805(p.38), 812, 856(#161).
Jerusalem	seal	ʾbʾ/bwnhy	525-475	50(p.65), 748(Ar89?), 810, 856(#160).
Jerusalem area	impression	ʾlntn	525-450	629(#5), 748(Ar36).
Jerusalem area	impression	yrmy	525-450	629(#6), 748(Ar37).
Jerusalem area	impression	brwk	525-450	629(#7), 748(Ar38).
Jerusalem area	impression	ygʾl	525-450	629(#8), 748(Ar39).
Jerusalem area	impression	ʾlʿzr	525-450	629(#9), 748(Ar40).
Jerusalem area	impression	šʾl	525-450	629(#10), 748(Ar41).

Index of Hebrew Personal Seals
(according to site)

Site	Artifact	"seal of..."	Date	Bibliographic Reference Number
Jerusalem area	impression	ʾlʿzr	525-450	629(#11), 748(Ar42).
Jerusalem area	impression	mykh	525-450	629(#12), 748(Ar43).
Jerusalem area	impression	šlmyt	525-450	629(#14), 748(Ar45).
Jerusalem area	seal	pšḥr	?	50(p.61), 846, 856(#148).
Jerusalem	seal	mnḥmt	?	24(#64), 41(t, p.11), 42(p.253), 714, 724, 733(#82), 771(p.44), 856(#64).
Khirbet Rabud	seal	šlm	750-700	759a.
Khirbet Yarmuk	impression	?	?	813.
Khirbet Yearim	seal	yšʿyhw	700-675	36a(#131), 655, 748(H49), 749(#75), 788, 805(pl.34), 856(#211).
Lachish	impression	šbnʾ	800-700	50(p.78), 273(p.46-47), 321(pl.47B:1), 748(H35); see also Ramat Raḥel, Tell en-Nasbeh for other occurrences of this impression.
Lachish	impression	šwk	750-700	50(p.78), 273(p.47-48), 748(H14).

Index of Hebrew Personal Seals
(according to site)

Site	Artifact	"seal of..."	Date	Bibliographic Reference Number
Lachish area	seal	ḥnh	725-675	662, 748(H155).
Lachish	impressions	ḥwšʿ	725-675	50(p.75-76), 273(p.40), 748(H15); see also Tell el-Judeideh for other occurrences of this impression.
Lachish	impression	ʿbdy	725-700	50(p.77-78), 273(p.38), 748(H16).
Lachish	impressions	spn	725-700	36a(#88), 50(p.73), 273(p.38), 275a, 304, 318, 330, 648(v.3, p.78), 748(H10), 749(#23), 855.
Lachish	impressions	nḥm	725-700	8(p.120), 36a(#90), 41a(v.1, p.183), 50(p.77), 61(v.3, p.1244), 273(p.44-45), 318, 594, 714, 748(H13), 749(#17).
Lachish	impression	ʿbdy	700-600	50(p.77-78), 273(p.45), 318.
Lachish	impression	nḥm	700-600	50(p.78-79), 275, 307, 318.
Lachish	seal	šbnʾ	700-650	24(#57), 35, 50(p.69), 273(pl.8.3), 288, 330, 648(v.1, p.195), 748(H20), 856(#57), 857(#57).
Lachish	impression	ḥlqyhw	675-625	50(p.62), 273(p.102), 275, 275a, 289, 304, 318, 321(p.348), 330, 748(H42), 749(#27), 805(p.39), 856(#150).
Lachish	seal	špṭyhw	675-625	36a(#125), 50(p.57), 273(p.103), 305, 306, 321(p.348), 330, 733(#67a), 748(H19), 749(#50), 805(p.33), 856(#109), 1199.

Index of Hebrew Personal Seals
(according to site)

Site	Artifact	"seal of..."	Date	Bibliographic Reference Number
Lachish	impressions	mšlm	675-625	50(p.76), 273(p.41), 318, 321(p.340), 648(v.3, p.78), 748(H11), 749(#14), 855.
Lachish	impressions	krmy	650-600	50(p.80), 273(p.51-52).
Lachish	impression	knbm(?)	650-600	50(p.80), 273(p.52-53).
Lachish	impression	rkʿš(?) dwdš(?)	650-600	50(p.81), 273(p.53-54).
Lachish	impression	smky	650-600	50(p.81), 273(p.54).
Lachish	impression	ṣpnyh	650-600	50(p.81), 273(p.45-55).
Lachish	impression	šlm(h)	650-600	50(p.76-77), 273(p.43), 275, 291a, 321(pl.47:A.9, 78.1, 78.5), 318, 855.
Lachish	seal	smk	650-600	35, 36a(#127), 50(p.58), 269, 273(p.102), 275, 289, 290, 318, 330, 332, 648(v.3, p.80), 733(#59), 748(H17), 749(#48), 805(p.35), 856(#139).
Lachish	impression	gdlyhw	650-600	35, 36a(#15), 50(p.61), 68a(p.223), 273(p.103) 290, 303, 303a, 306, 318, 321(p.347), 330, 648(v.2, p.441; v.3, p.80), 748(H18), 781, 856(#149), 857(#149), 858, 866.
Lachish	seal	šlm	650-600	273(p.104), 318.
Lachish	impression	šlm	650-600	50(p.63), 273(p.38, 104), 318, 748(H19).

Index of Hebrew Personal Seals
(according to site)

Site	Artifact	"seal of..."	Date	Bibliographic Reference Number
Lachish	impression	pn	650-600	50(p.79-80), 273(p.51).
Lachish	impressions	tnḥm	650-600	50(p.76), 273(p.41-42), 275, 318, 321(p.341), 748(H12), 855; see also Gibeon, Ramat Raḥel for other occurrences of this impression.
Lachish	impression	nryhw	625-600	36a(#29), 260, 748(H25), 857(#255).
Lachish	impression	šbnyhw	625-600	36a(#26), 50(p.79), 260, 273(p.50), 275, 318, 748(H26).
Lachish	impression	yhwʾl	625-600	36a(#30), 260, 748(H21), 857(#256).
Lachish	impression	yhwkl	625-600	36a(#27), 260, 748(H22), 856(#253).
Lachish	impression	yrmyhw	625-600	36a(#31), 260, 748(H23), 857(#258).
Lachish	impression	nḥm	625-600	36a(#28), 260, 748(H24), 857(#254).
Lachish	impression	š...šbnyh	?	50(p.79), 273(p.49).
Megiddo	seal	šmʿ	750	24(#68), 35, 36a(#18), 50(p.70), 331, 335(p.99), 699, 711, 733(#17), 748(H1), 749(#3), 801, 805(p.27), 856(#68), 857(#68), 871.
Megiddo	seal	ʾsp	750-700	24(#7), 35, 41a(v.3, p.45), 61(v.2, p.1286), 331, 335, 337(p.99), 648(v.1, p.483), 661, 748(H156), 772, 856(#7), 857(#7).

130

Index of Hebrew Personal Seals
(according to site)

Site	Artifact	"seal of..."	Date	Bibliographic Reference Number
Megiddo	seal	ḥmn	700-650	24(#3), 36a(#126), 50(p.66), 333(pl.67:10), 336, 338, 648(v.3, p.80), 733(#2), 748(H43), 749(#42), 761, 805(p.31), 840, 856(#3).
Megiddo	seal	ʾlʾmr	700-650	50(p.56), 733(#15), 748(P19), 780, 856(#136).
Nablus	seal	pqḥ	775-725	24(#4), 42(p.353), 50(p.66), 703(#5), 714, 733(#137), 748(H56), 856(#4), 857(#4).
Nablus	seal	ḥgy	?	24(#2), 42(p.270), 648(v.3, p.27), 703(#6), 714, 733(#133), 856(#2).
Nebi Rubin	seal/weight	brky	500-300?	738a, 856(#193), 857(193).
Ramat Raḥel	impression	šbnʾ	800-700	36a(#86), 340(v.2, pl.40.2, 40.3), 648(v.3, p.78); 748(H35), 788, 856(#223); see also Lachish, Tell en-Nasbeh for other occurrences of this impression.
Ramat Raḥel	impression	ʾhyw	800-700	339, 856(#183).
Ramat Raḥel	impression	mnḥm	775-725	36(#89), 339, 340(v.1, pl.6.4), 341, 343, 748(H30), 749(#21), 856(#197), 857(#197).
Ramat Raḥel	impression	ʾlyqm	725-700	36a(#22,23), 340(v.2, pl.40.4), 748(H31), 749(#9), 781; see also Beth Shemesh, Tell Beit Mirsim for other occurences of this impression.
Ramat Raḥel	impression	yhwḥl	725-675	36a(#87), 340(v.1, pl.27.2), 341, 748(H32), 749(#20), 788, 856(#198).

Index of Hebrew Personal Seals
(according to site)

Site	Artifact	"seal of..."	Date	Bibliographic Reference Number
Ramat Raḥel	impression	yhwḥl	725-675	340(v.1, pl.27.1), 341, 748(H33), 803, 856(#198).
Ramat Raḥel	impression	nrʾ	725-700	340(v.1, p.16), 749(#18).
Ramat Raḥel	impression	tnḥm	650-600	340(v.2, pl.40.5), 748(H12), 855; see also Gibeon, Lachish for other occurrences of this impression.
Ramat Raḥel	impression	nrʾ	625-600	340(v.1, pl.6.2), 341, 748(H34), 788, 803, 856(#196).
Ramat Raḥel	impression	...tbrʾ	?	340(v.2, pl.32.33-60), 788, 856(#222).
Ramat Raḥel	impression	...ʾlsmʿ	?	340(v.2, pl.32.33-60), 788, 856(#224).
Samaria	seal	ʾbʾhy	800-700	399(p.247), 856(#105).
Samaria	seal	šmryw	800-775	36a(#39), 748(H67), 749(#35), 788, 827, 856(#214).
Samaria	seal	šr	800-700	24(#99), 407, 748(H68), 842, 856(#99).
Samaria	seal	pṭʾs	800-700	50(p.55), 350, 748(Ar48), 749(#41), 805(p.31), 856(#134).
Samaria	seal	sdq	750-700	641(pl.10), 748(H57).
Samaria	impression	yprʿyw	750-700	653, 748(H69), 808, 856(#177).

Index of Hebrew Personal Seals
(according to site)

Site	Artifact	"seal of..."	Date	Bibliographic Reference Number
Samaria(?)	seal	ꜣlyṣr	700-675	652, 748(H75).
Samaria	seal	klm	?	359(p.87), 856(#185).
Shechem	seal	mbn	650-600	420, 422, 423(fig.91), 748(H51), 788, 856(#206), 857(#206), 872a.
Tell Beit Mirsim	impression	ꜣlyqm	725-700	24(#9), 35, 36a(#22,23), 50(p.82), 556(v.1, p.78), 557-560, 625, 626, 713, 748(H31), 749(#8), 759, 781, 866; see also Beth Shemesh, Ramat Raḥel for other occurrences of this impression.
Tell el-Farah(S)	seal	ḥym	725-650	24(#8), 50(p.66), 733(#7), 748(H159), 749(#3), 761, 805(p.32), 856(#8), 921a(p.10).
Tell el-Ḥesi	impression	mtnyhw	650-575	790.
Tell el-Judeideh	impressions	nḥm	725-700	36a(#90), 748(H3), 749(#17); see also Lachish for other occurrences of this impression.
Tell el-Judeideh	impression	hwšꜥ	725-675	8(p.119), 41a(v.1, p.183), 61(v.3, p.1244), 714, 749(#22); see also Lachish for other occurrences of this impression.
Tell el-Judeideh(?)	impression	mnḥm	725-675	50(p.74), 107(v.5, p.82), 748(H53).
Tell el-Judeideh	impression	šbnyhw	725-700	8(p.120), 41a(v.1, p.183), 61(v.3, p.1244), 594, 714, 748(H65), 749(#24).

Index of Hebrew Personal Seals
(according to site)

Site	Artifact	"seal of..."	Date	Bibliographic Reference Number
Tell el-Judeideh	impression	šlm	700-600	50(p.83), 667, 748(H66), 749(#15), 856(#120, 121), 857(#121).
Tell el-Judeideh	impression	mšlm(?)	700-600	675.
Tell el-Judeideh	seal	mʿsyhw	700-600	24(#55), 648(v.5, p.204), 856(#55).
Tell en-Nasbeh	impression	šbnʾ	800-700	586(p.163), 748(H35), 749(#19), see also Lachish, Ramat Raḥel for other occurrences of this impression.
Tell en-Nasbeh	impression	ʾhzyhw	700-600	50(p.81-82), 586(p.163), 748(H37).
Tell en-Nasbeh	seal	yʾznyhw	650-600	6(#19,20), 24(#69), 35, 36a(#19), 50(p.70), 582, 586(p.163), 648(v.3, p.80), 733(#43), 738, 748(H46), 749(#5), 781, 805(p.36), 856(#69), 857(#69).
Tell eṣ-Ṣafi	impression	rpʾ	750-700	748(H63).
Tell eṣ-Ṣafi	impression	rpty	750-650	8(p.121), 41a(v.1, p.55), 61(v.3, p.1244), 594, 597, 689, 714, 820.
Tell eṣ-Ṣafi	impression	yhwʿz	700-675	50(p.64), 748(H47), 749(#89), 812, 856(#156).
Tell eṣ-Soda	seal	ntnyhw	775-725	24(#32), 42(p.327), 50(p.68), 714, 720, 724(#35), 733(#38), 748(H121), 770, 771(p.35), 856(#32).

Index of Hebrew Personal Seals
(according to site)

Site	Artifact	"seal of..."	Date	Bibliographic Reference Number
Tell es-Soda	seal	nḥmyhw	750-700	13(pl.13.6), 24(#30), 42(p.308), 648(v.4, p.880), 703(#42), 714, 748(H119).
Tell Jemmeh	seal	drymš	800-750	24(#93), 50(p.71), 648(v.1, p.351), 713, 732, 791a, 856(#93), 870.
Tell Qasile	seal	ʿsnyhw	700-600	50(p.52), 589, 856(#125), 857(#125), 902, 921.
Tell Sandahannah	impression	šbnyhw	?	24(#5), 41a(v.1, p.183), 594.
Tell Zakaria	impression	ʿzr	500-300	8(p.21, 123), 41a(v.1, p.179), 61(v.3, p.1244), 156, 158, 592, 687, 714, 820.
Tell Zakaria	seal	ʾz(?)	?	24(#78), 593, 598, 856(#78).
Tell Zakaria	impression	špn	?	8(p.121), 41a(v.1, p.179), 61(v.3, p.1244), 592, 594, 714, 820.
Trans-Jordan	seal	ʾlsmky	625-575	648(v.3, p.80), 748(P11), 805(p.28), 810.
Umm el-Qanafid	seal	ʾgl	625-600	731.

Index of Hebrew Personal Seals
(unknown provenance)

"seal of..."	Date	Bibliographic Reference Number
ʾbgd	800-775	644, 748(H71), 749(#127), 787, 856(#234).
ʾbyw	725-700	50(p.56), 648(v.1, p.23), 733(#182), 748(H72), 749(#36), 805(p.28), 810, 856(#123), 857(#123).
ʾbyw	?	24(#65), 41(n, p.11), 42(p.205), 50(p.69), 61(v.3, p.1861), 648(v.1, p.23), 674, 703(#1), 714, 724, 733(#85), 757, 771(p.41), 856(#65), 857(#65).
ʾbšwʿ	?	24(#1), 42(p.206), 648(v.1, p.34), 703(#11), 714, 856(#1).
ʾḥʾmh	700-600	678(#8).
ʾḥz	?	24(#44), 42(p.206), 61(v.3, p.1264), 714, 733(#8), 838, 856(#44), 857(#44).
ʾḥyhw	750-700	633(#12), 748(H73), 749(#87), 856(#246).
ʾḥymn	?	50(p.54), 275a.
ʾḥmlk	700-600	50(p.52), 648(v.3, p.80), 733(#59), 748(H146), 805(p.32), 838, 840, 856(#124).
ʾḥtmlk	?	24(#63), 42(p.213), 50(p.69), 714, 724, 733(#144), 771(p.38), 856(#63), 857(#63).
ʾyʿdh	625-600	50(p.62), 648(v.3, p.80), 748(H147), 749(#52), 750, 810(p.114), 856(#151).
ʾldqn	725-700	621a(pl.30), 748(H160).
ʾldlh	750-700	50(p.58-59), 659, 748(H74), 856(#140).
ʾlzkr	?	24(#42), 61(v.3, p.1867), 717, 824, 856(#42).

Index of Hebrew Personal Seals
(unknown provenance)

"seal of..."	Date	Bibliographic Reference Number
ʾlḥnn	?	24(#5), 41a(v.1, p.274), 50(p.66), 61(v.1, p.243), 648(v.1, p.334), 733(#75), 856(#5).
ʾlyqm (impression)	750-700	633(#8), 748(H76), 749(#26), 856(#242).
ʾlyqm	700-600	749(#91).
ʾlyšb	725-650	678(#17).
ʾlntn	700-600	50(p.57-58), 748(Ar110), 805(p.34), 811, 856(#138), 857(#138).
ʾlrm	725-675	15(v.2, p.74), 42(p.21), 703(#25), 714, 748(H153), 779, 788, 856(#220), 857(#220).
ʾlrm (Ammonite?)	?	13(pl.9.5), 24(#94), 678(p.57), 733(#126), 748(Ar27), 856(#94).
ʾlšmʿ	675-625	24(#100), 41a(v.3, p.46), 61(v.2, p.866), 648(v.1, p.355), 720, 748(H152), 818, 856(#100), 862.
ʾlšmʿ	700-675	24(#72), 50(p.70), 648(v.3, p.80), 694, 733(#65), 748(H148), 818, 819, 847, 856(#72), 857(#72).
ʾny	?	24(#80), 703(#49), 733(#6), 856(#80).
ʾply	700-675	633(#11), 748(H77), 749(#70), 856(#245).
ʾprḥ	625-575	633(#5), 748(H78), 749(#88), 856(#239), 857(#239).

Index of Hebrew Personal Seals
(unknown provenance)

"seal of..."	Date	Bibliographic Reference Number
ᵓprḥ	650-550	749(#51).
ᵓṣyh	?	24(#97), 41a(v.1, p.15), 42(p.486), 61(v.3, p.928), 698, 856(#97), 857(#97).
ᵓryhw	775-725	652(pl.1), 748(H79).
ᵓryhw	725-675	749(#79).
ᵓryhw	600-500	749(#80).
ᵓšyhw	725-675	678(#12).
ᵓšnᵓ	725-700	35, 50(p.59), 648(v.1, p.207), 733(#1a), 748(H2), 844, 845, 848, 851, 853(v.1, p.64), 856(#141), 857(#141).
ᵓšnᵓ	750-650	749(#40).
blgy	?	50(p.60), 648(v.2, p.131), 846, 856(#143).
blgy	625-575	652(pl.1), 748(H80).
bn	700-675	24(#89), 41a(v.1, p.277), 61(v.1, p.65), 704, 733(#66), 748(H81), 856(#89), 857(#89).
bnyhw	750-700	621a(pl.30), 748(H123).
bnyhw	675-625	656(fig.12), 748(H82).
bnyhw	?	24(#18), 42(p.238), 714, 752, 770, 771(p.27), 856(#18).

138

Index of Hebrew Personal Seals
(unknown provenance)

"seal of..."	Date	Bibliographic Reference Number
bnyhw	700-600	749(#82).
bsy	750-650	633(#13), 748(Ar51), 749(#38), 856(#247), 857(#247).
brkyhw (impression)	625-600	628, 635, 708a.
gdyhw (gryhw)	675-625	50(p.59), 748(H83), 749(#63), 805(p.38), 810, 856(#142), 857(#142).
gdlyhw	625-600	36a(#128), 633(#6), 748(H84), 749(#49), 856(#240).
dlh	725-700	633(#4), 748(H85), 749(#39), 856(#238).
dlh (impression)	?	678(#22).
dml'	700-600	640, 749(#47).
dmlyhw (rmlyhw)	?	711, 818.
h'mn	?	24(#101), 41a(v.1, p.12), 61(v.1, p.64), 704, 714, 748(Ar14), 856(#101).
hwdyhw	725-650	678(#1b).
hwdyhw	725-650	678(#9).
hwš‘	750-700	728, 748(H86), 856(#181), 857(#181).

Index of Hebrew Personal Seals
(unknown provenance)

"seal of..."	Date	Bibliographic Reference Number
hwšʿyhw	625-575	749(#72).
hwšʿyhw	650-550	749(#73), 750.
hwšʿyhw	675-625	36a(#132), 50(p.60), 648(v.3, p.80), 805(p.37), 810.
hnmy	?	24(#90), 42(p.260), 733(#119), 771(p.16), 856(#90).
hṣlyhw	700-600	749(#59).
hṣlyhw	725-675	749(#60).
zkr	650-600	24(#47), 42(p.169,268,338), 50(p.69), 681a(#2511), 703(#4), 714, 733(#36), 748(H144), 856(#47).
zkr	775-725	14(p.362), 24(#46), 41(h,p.11), 41a(v.1, p.141,274), 61(v.3, p.1862), 648(v.2, p.920), 703, 704a, 714, 724, 733(#10), 748(H89), 771(p.42), 795, 856(#46), 857(#46).
zkryhw	?	24(#104), 648(v.2, p.922), 856(#104), 857(#104).
zryw(?)	900-800	61a, 748(H161).
ḥgy	700-650	657, 748(H70), 788, 856(#203).
ḥwrṣ	725-700	24(#22), 41a(v.1, p.274), 42(p.504), 61(v.2, p.932; v.3, p.1855), 670a, 706, 714, 748(H90), 769, 856(#22).
ḥwnn	?	24(#21), 50(p.67), 748(UD7), 847, 856(#21), 857(#21).

Index of Hebrew Personal Seals
(unknown provenance)

"seal of..."	Date	Bibliographic Reference Number
ḥymn	?	50(#7), 648(v.1, p.218), 733(#118), 856(#130).
ḥlqyhw	725-675	749(#55), 750.
ḥlqyhw	700-600	749(#56).
ḥmyʿdn	700-600	640, 749(#33).
ḥnn	?	24(#49), 41a(v.2, p.145), 61(v.2, p.615), 688, 697, 856(#49).
ḥnn	725-675	633(#3), 748(H91), 856(#237).
ḥnn	?	24(#91), 41a(v.1, p.10,277), 61(v.1, p.60), 704, 733(#58), 748(Ar107?, UD4?), 856(#91).
ḥnnyh	725-675	24(#33), 42(p.278), 714, 724, 748(Ar64), 771(p.36), 856(#23).
ḥnnyhw (impression)	600-575	649, 655, 748(H92), 788, 856(#218), 857(#218).
ḥnnyhw	625-600	24(#24), 42(p.278), 50(p.67), 703(#2), 714, 720, 733(#78), 748(H93), 795, 856(#24), 857(#24).
ḥnnyhw	675-625	24(#25), 42(p.278), 50(p.68), 703(#1), 714, 720, 733(#76), 748(H94), 795, 856(#25).
ḥṣy	675-625	650, 748(H95), 808, 856(#169).
ṭbʾ	725-700	678(#18).

141

Index of Hebrew Personal Seals
(unknown provenance)

"seal of..."	Date	Bibliographic Reference Number
yʾznyhw	625-575	633(#7), 748(H96), 856(#241), 857(#241).
yhwʾḥz	650-600	36a(#20), 633(#21), 748(H97), 749(#6), 856(#252), 857(#252).
yhwyšmʿ	625-600	649a, 748(H98), 789, 856(#226), 857(#226), 858a.
yhwʿzr	600-575	24(#26), 41(b, p.10), 41a(v.1, p.15; v.2, p.145), 50(p.68), 61(v.1, p.487), 697, 698, 733(#37), 714, 748(H99), 850, 852, 856(#26).
yhwʿzr	700-600	749(#61).
yhwqm	600-500	640, 749(#92).
yhwšʿ (impression)	675-625	24(#27), 648(v.3, p.542), 748(H100), 852.
ywʾb	?	24(#9), 41a(v.3, p.46), 42(p.288), 61(v.2, p.556), 670, 714, 733(#97), 771(p.45), 856(#9), 857(#9).
ywʾmn	700-650	650, 748(H101), 856(#172).
ywʾr	725-700	633(#15), 748(H102), 856(#249).
ywznb	750-700	678(#13).
ywʿšh	700-675	650, 748(H103), 856(#171).
yzbl	850-750	35, 36a(#40), 645, 748(P6), 788, 856(#215), 857(#215).

Index of Hebrew Personal Seals
(unknown provenance)

"seal of..."	Date	Bibliographic Reference Number
yzn'l	?	24(#28), 42(p.217), 50(#68), 714, 724, 733(#142), 771(p.26), 856(#28).
yḥzq	?	24(#83), 42(p.287), 50(#71), 56(p.658), 703(#7), 733(#11), 856(#83).
yhmlyhw	675-625	24(#51), 41(e, p.11), 42(p.287,315), 50(p.69), 648(v.3, p.80), 693a, 720, 733(#64), 748(H149), 838, 856(#51), 857(#51).
yhṣ	800-775	24(#10), 50(p.67), 727, 733(#81), 748(H104), 805(p.37), 856(#10).
ykl	?	24(#66), 42(p.206,259), 50(p.70), 681a(#2519), 703(#12), 714, 748(Ar82), 856(#66).
y'dr'l	?	24(#84), 42(p.289), 703(#13), 733(#50), 856(#24).
yqmyhw	725-675	50(p.54), 648(v.3, p.80), 665, 748(H105), 749(#44), 805(p.33), 856(#122).
yqmyhw	?	24(#53), 232, 648(v.3, p.80) 856(#53).
yr'	750-700	650, 748(H106), 856(#173).
yr'wyhw	600-500	640, 749(#95).
yrḥm'l (impression)	625-600	628, 635, 708a.
yrymwt	700-600	678(#3).
yrm	675-625	24(#54), 35, 41(g, p.11), 41a(v.1, p.11), 50(p.69), 648(v.2, p.932), 704, 714, 733(#67), 745, 748(H107), 856(#54), 857(#54).
yrmyhw	725-650	678(#6).

Index of Hebrew Personal Seals
(unknown provenance)

"seal of..."	Date	Bibliographic Reference Number
yrmyhw	775–725	36a(#129), 633(#14), 748(H108), 749(#45), 856(#248).
yšmʿʾl	725–675	749(#57).
yšʿyhw	?	24(#52), 61(v.2, p.880), 648(v.3, p.161), 736, 856(#52), 857(#52).
yšʿ	?	24(#85), 41a(v.1, p.10,24), 61(v.1, p.61), 704, 714, 733(#72), 748(Ar21), 856(#85).
klklyhw	650–550	640, 749(#93).
kšy	675–625	652, 748(H109).
lhṣ	750–650	633(#17), 748(UD2), 856(#251).
mʾš	675–625	677, 748(H110).
myʾmn	650–550	749(#94).
mky	625–575	50(p.63), 652a, 648(v.4, p.959), 748(H111), 810(p.115), 856(#153), 857(#153).
mky	600–500	652a, 749(#84), 810(p.115).
mkyhw	725–650	678(#10).
mlkyhw	675–625	648(v.4, p.1129), 748(H112), 808, 856(#176).
mlkyhw	675–625	656, 748(H113).
mlkyhw	725–675	640, 749(#68).

144

Index of Hebrew Personal Seals
(unknown provenance)

"seal of.."	Date	Bibliographic Reference Number
mlkrm	700-600	633(#16), 748(P8), 856(#250).
mnḥ	?	24(#11), 42(p.305), 648(v.5, p.14), 856(#11).
mnḥm	650-550	749(#78).
mnḥm	725-700	749(#46).
mnḥm	700-675	728, 748(Ar47), 856(#142), 857(#142).
mnḥm	?	647a, 648(v.5, p.40), 788, 856(#195), 857(#195).
mnḥm (impression)	?	8(p.120), 41a(v.1, p.183), 61(v.3, p.1244), 594, 708, 714.
mnšh	725-675	35, 652a, 648(v.5, p.40), 748(H114), 788, 856(#209), 857(#209).
mʿšyhw	700-600	749(#77).
mqnyhw	675-625	50(p.65), 137, 648(v.5, p.360), 748(H116), 856(#162).
mtn	700-600	678(#16).
mttyhw	700-600	627a, 629a.
nʾhbt	625-600	24(#60), 41(q, p.11), 42(p.320,369), 714, 748(H117), 770, 771(p.46), 815, 847, 856(#60).
nḥm	700-650	657, 748(#118), 856(#202), 857(#202).
nḥm	725-675	633(#10), 748(H157), 749(#71), 856(#244).

Index of Hebrew Personal Seals
(unknown provenance)

"seal of..."	Date	Bibliographic Reference Number
nn(?)	650-550?	24(#76), 714, 724, 748(P9?), 771(p.42), 856(#76).
nʿmʾl	?	24(#95), 42(p.324), 61(v.3, p.1914), 714, 733(#53), 856(#95).
nry	800-700	50(p.53), 727, 856(#127).
nryhw	?	24(#56), 816, 856(#56).
ntnyhw	675-625	24(#31), 648(v.4, p.988), 748(H120), 847, 856(#31).
sylʾ	725-675	50(p.63), 748(H122), 749(#69), 811, 856(#155).
smk	700-600	749(#83).
sryh	?	24(#33), 42(p.238,331), 50(p.68), 714, 724, 771(p.37), 856(#33).
strh	?	24(#12), 648(v.5, p.1130), 733(#68), 847, 856(#12).
ʿbdʾlʾb	?	14(p.362), 24(#73), 42(p.320,332,357,372), 50(p.70), 648(v.5, p.678), 673, 703(p.145), 714, 771(p.39,54), 856(#73).
ʿbdyhw	650-600	24(#35), 41a(v.2, p.70), 61(v.1, p.323), 696, 700, 707, 708, 714, 748(H124), 856(#35).
ʿbdyhw	675-625	24(#34), 42(p.291), 681a(#2518), 714, 748(H145), 770, 771(p.46), 856(#34).
ʿbdyhw	?	24(#70), 35, 41(m,p.11), 42(p.334), 61(v.2, p.864; v.3, p.1866), 700, 824, 856(#70), 857(#70).
ʿbdyhw	650-550	749(#74), 750.

Index of Hebrew Personal Seals
(unknown provenance)

"seal of..."	Date	Bibliographic Reference Number
ʿbdkyn	?	24(#87), 41a(v.2, p.147), 50(p.71), 61(v.2, p.616), 697, 733(#52), 856(#87).
ʿbyw	550-500	748(Ar30), 808, 856(#174).
ʿdyhw	725-650	678(#14).
ʿzʾ	700-675	648(v.3, p.80), 653, 748(H125), 808, 856(#179).
ʿzʾ	?	24(#36), 42(p-240), 648(v.2, p.288; v.3, p.80), 653, 714, 724, 771(p.45), 856(#36).
ʿzʾl	550-500	657, 748(Ar31), 856(#200).
ʿzyhw	700-600	749(#65).
ʿzyhw	?	24(#37), 41(c,p.11), 41a(v.1, p.274), 61(v.3, p.1864), 648(v.3, p.289), 705, 714, 768, 856(#37), 857(#37).
ʿzr	725-650	678(#11).
ʿzryh	600-500	808, 856(#175), 857(#175).
ʿzryhw	600-550	748(H126), 808.
ʿzryhw	625-600	678(#4).
ʿzryhw	625-600	652, 748(H128).
ʿzryw	725-700	35, 634, 748(H127), 789, 856(#228), 857(#228).

147

Index of Hebrew Personal Seals
(unknown provenance)

"seal of..."	Date	Bibliographic Reference Number
ʿkbr	725–700	655, 748(H129), 788, 856(#210), 857(#210).
ʿmdyhw	700–675	24(#61), 41(p.11), 41a(v.2, p.70), 50(p.69), 61(v.1, p.322), 696, 707, 708, 714, 748(H143), 856(#61).
ʿšy	725–675	633(#9), 748(H130), 749(#62), 856(#243).
ʿšyhw	750–650	678(#7).
ʿšyw	725–700	13(pl.9.27), 14(p.362), 24(#38), 35, 42(p.287,346), 50(p.68), 648(v.3, p.526), 714, 733(#84), 748(H131), 771(p.54), 856(#38), 857(#38).
pdh	700–650	633(#2), 748(Ar52), 856(#236).
plʾyh	700–600	627a, 629a.
pdyhw	625–600	633(#1), 748(H132), 856(#235), 857(#235).
plṭyhw (impression)	750–650	678(#21).
pmn	600–500	648(v.3, p.80), 653, 856(#180).
prʿ	?	50(p.53), 350, 811, 856(#126).
spn	650–550	749(#90).
spn	700–600	678(#2).
qlyhw	700–675	748(H133), 753, 800, 856(#233).
qsr	?	24(96), 42(p.364), 703(#45), 856(#96).

Index of Hebrew Personal Seals
(unknown provenance)

"seal of..."	Date	Bibliographic Reference Number
rpʾ	750-650	678(#19).
...bn rpʾ	?	678(#20).
śryhw	600-575	628, 647.
šʾl	?	24(#92), 41a(v.1, p.277; v.2, p.146), 856(#92), 857(#92).
šʾl	750-700	35, 648(v.3, p.80), 653, 748(H142), 856(#178), 857(#178).
šby	?	24(#43), 717, 824, 856(#43).
šbnʾ	700-650	650, 748(H134), 856(#168).
šbnyhw	750-700	723.
šbnyhw	800-750	24(#67), 41(o.p.11), 42(p.338,372), 50(p.70), 714, 720, 722(#A1147), 723, 733(#125), 748(H4), 757, 771(p.39), 856(#67), 857(#67), 980.
šhrhr	700-675	24(#39), 42(p.359,374), 61(v.3, p.1871), 703(#41), 707, 708, 714, 748(H135), 856(#39), 857(#39).
šlm	?	24(#58), 41a(v.1, p.275), 61(v.3, p.1865), 704a, 714, 856(#58), 857(#58).
šlm	?	24(#75), 50(p.70), 796, 856(#75), 857(#75).
šlm	725-650	678(#15).
šlmʾl	?	50(p.60), 748(Ar26), 810, 856(#145).

Index of Hebrew Personal Seals
(unknown provenance)

"seal of..."	Date	Bibliographic Reference Number
šmʾb	750-650	50(p.53), 648(v.3, p.80), 748(Ar62), 805(p.28), 806, 811, 856(#128).
šmʿ	675-625	24(#16), 42(p.378), 50(p.67), 703(#9), 733(#3), 748(H137), 856(#16).
šmʿ	?	24(#71), 41(1,p.11), 41a(v.2, p.140), 61(v.2, p.614), 686, 711, 720, 856(#71), 857(#71).
šmʿ	725-675	650, 748(H138), 856(#167), 857(#167).
šmʿyhw	?	24(#40), 35, 41(a,p.10), 42(p.338), 50(p.68), 714, 720, 724, 733(#31), 771(p.34), 856(#40), 857(#40).
šmr	?	733(#56), 856(#106).
šmryhw	725-650	678(#5).
šnyw	?	50(p.55), 748(UD3), 810, 856(#132).
šʿybb	775-725	649, 748(H139), 788, 856(#216).
šʿl	775-725	652, 748(H140), 749(#76).
šʿnp	700-600	640, 749(#85).
šʿryhw	725-650	678(#1a).
špṭ	800-700	36a(#124), 50(p.57), 666, 667, 748(H141), 749(#37), 805(p.29), 856(#137), 857(#137).

Index of Hebrew Personal Seals
(unknown provenance)

"seal of..."	Date	Bibliographic Reference Number
ˇspṭyhw	650-550	749(#96).
ˇsʔlqy (impression)	700-600	678(#23).

151

Index of Royal, Provincial and City Seals

Site	Artifact	Inscription	Date	Bibliographic Reference Number
Aro'er	impressions	lmlk	?	672.
Bethany	impressions	yhd, yršlm	300-100	921b.
En Gedi	impression	lmlk	650-600	782, 910a.
En Gedi	impression	yhwd	500-300	910a.
Gezer	impressions	lmlk	725-600	152, 153, 171.
Gezer	impressions	yhwd	500-300	152, 153, 776, 876.
Gibeon	impressions	lmlk	700-600	191-197.
Jericho	impression	yhwd	500-300	201, 205, 638, 876.
Jericho	impressions	sgnd/hgr/ yhwd	500-300	201, 203-205, 638, 719, 856(#184).
Jerusalem	impressions	lmlk	800-600	220, 224, 237, 630, 687, 834, 835.
Jerusalem	impressions	yhwd/yh	500-300	742, 783(p.64), 834, 835, 860, 876.
Jerusalem	impressions	yršlm	400-200	234, 244, 627, 783(p.64), 834, 835.

*For the early discussions of the royal seal impressions, consult Bibliographic Reference Numbers 24(p.155-157), 50(p.92-98).
For the early discussions of the provincial and city seal impressions, consult Bibliographic Reference Number 24(p.136-137 and following).
Comprehensive articles on the royal, provincial and city seal impressions may be found under Bibliographic Reference Numbers 624, 629, 689, 703, 709, 719, 725, 762, 764, 765, 766a, 767, 775, 777, 786, 794, 804, 817, 833, 843, 854, 856, 857, 863, 867-869.

Index of Royal, Provincial and City Seals

Site	Artifact	Inscription	Date	Bibliographic Reference Number
Judea	impressions	yh/yhwd	600-500	629.
Judea	impressions	sr hʿr	625-600	632, 658.
Khirbet Rabud	impressions	lmlk	750-700	759a.
Lachish	impressions	lmlk	650-600	272, 273, 326a, 855.
Lachish	impression	yršlm	650-600	273, 275.
Ramat Rahel	impressions	yhwd	500-300	339, 340, 621, 719, 876.
Tell Beit Mirsim	impressions	lmlk	750-600	556, 855.
Tell en-Nasbeh	impressions	lmlk	750-600	580, 586.
Tell en-Nasbeh	impressions	yhd, yršlm	500-300	580, 586, 876.
Tell en-Nasbeh	impressions	mṣh/mwṣh	500-300	580, 581, 586, 639, 710, 895.
Tell eṣ-Ṣafi	impressions	lmlk	770-600	8.
Tell Zakaria	impressions	lmlk	700-600	592, 597, 680, 690, 820.

153

Index of Inscribed Weights and Measures

Site	Artifact	Inscription	Date	Bibliographic Reference Number
ʿAnata area	weight	nṣp	?	61(v.3, p.1250), 684, 691, 797, 798, 821.
Ascalon	weight	šql	?	50, 809, 809a.
Beth-Zur	weights	bqʿ,nṣp,pym	700-600	831(fig.53-54), 832.
En Gedi	weights	-1-	700-600	910a(pl.26.2).
Gerar	weights	nṣp,pym	700-600	791(p.45).
Gezer	weights	bqʿ,nṣp,pym	700-600	61(v.3, p.1253-1260), 126, 158(fig.431-432), 163, 720a, 797, 798, 801a.
Gezer	bronze weight	lmlk	700-600	158(fig.433).
Jerusalem	weights	bqʿ,nṣp,pym	650-590	41a(v.2, p.148; v.3, p.47), 61(v.3, p.1253-1261), 219, 239, 662a, 663, 720a, 797, 798, 801a, 849, 881.
Jerusalem	bronze weight	lzkryhw yʾr	?	24(#104), 797.
Judea	weights	bqʿ,nṣp,pym	800-600	826.
Khirbet el-Kom	weights	pym	700-600	250.

*Collections of weights and comprehensive articles on weights can be found under Bibliographic Reference Numbers 4a, 24, 35, 50, 267, 268, 657a, 664, 664a, 720a, 791, 792, 797, 798, 809, 830.

Index of Inscribed Weights and Measures

Site	Artifact	Inscription	Date	Bibliographic Reference Number
Lachish	weights	bqʿ,nṣp,pym	650-600	50, 274, 321(pl.51).
Lachish	measures	bt lmlk	650-600	35, 273, 291a, 330, 843.
Nebi Rubin	seal/weight	lbrky	500-300?	738a, 856(#193), 857(#193).
Petra	bronze weight	ḥmšt	?	793a.
Ramat Rahel	weights	bqʿ	700-600	340.
Samaria	weight	rbʿšl	?	351-353, 361, 401, 402, 684, 760, 797, 798, 814, 819, 821.
Silwan	weight	pym	?	61(v.3, p.1258), 794a, 801a, 830a.
Suse	measures	hn l wḥzy	750-600	41a(v.3, p.47), 61(v.2, p.665), 660, 685, 692, 836.
Tell Beit Mirsim	measures	bt	?	557, 560, 660.
Tell en-Nasbeh	weights	nṣp,pym	700-600	50, 586(p.259-260).
Tell Zakaria	weights	bqʿ,ksp,nṣp	?	8(p.145), 61(v.3, p.1251), 593, 595, 597, 684, 690, 797, 798.
Several Sites	weights	fractions of a sheqel	800-600	41a(v.1, p.13), 61(v.1, p.70), 828.

Index of Inscribed Weights and Measures

Site	Artifact	Inscription	Date	Bibliographic Reference Number
Several Sites	weights	numerals	?	622.
Several Sites	weights	sheqel sign	800-600	829.
?	weights	bqʿ	?	622, 833a, 881.
?	weight	ksp	?	691.
?	bronze weight	lmgn	700-600	881.
?	weight	1smʿ	800-700	642.
?	measure	hn	800-700	1144.
?	weights	nṣp, pym	?	835a.

Index of Ammonite Personal Seals (according to site)

Site	Artifact	"seal of..."	Date	Bibliographic Reference Number
Amman	seal	šbʾl	800-750	729, 746(pl.6), 748(A23), 856(#165), 857(#165).
Amman	seal	mnḥm	725-700	729, 746(pl.6), 748(A20), 856(#166), 857(#166), 940, 960.
Amman	seal	plṭy	700-600	749(#109).
Amman(?)	seal	ndbʾl	700-600(?)	24(#29), 41a(v.3, p.279), 50(p.68), 61(v.2, p.881; v.3, p.1489), 856(#29), 859.
Amman	seal	ʾdnnr	675-650	648(v.3, p.80), 746(pl.6), 729, 748(A1), 856(#164), 857(#164), 940, 960.
Amman	seal	ʾlʾmṣ	625-600	10(v.2, p.45), 61(#1888), 748(A5), 838, 856(#115), 857(#115).
Amman	seal	ʾltsʿ	625-600	748(A32), 856(#117), 857(#117), 948.
Amman	seal	ʾwʾ	625-600	748(A16), 788, 856(#194), 857(#194), 953, 960.
Amman	seal	ʿlyh	625-600	50(p.64), 643, 648(v.3, p.80), 748(A12), 749(#28), 805(p.39), 812, 856(#157), 857(#157), 960.
Baqdad	seal	šʿl	625-600	24(#41), 50(p.68), 648(v.1, p.358), 713, 716, 733(#28), 734, 748(A15), 749(#108), 856(#41).
Irbid	seal	ʿnmwt	600-575	748(A13), 749(#29), 805(p.43), 856(#116), 857(#116).
Tell es-Salt	seal	bydʾl	?	24(#17), 61(v.2, p.879), 736, 856(#17).

Index of Ammonite Personal Seals (unknown provenance)

"seal of..."	Date	Bibliographic Reference Number
ʾbgdhw	700–600	678(#37).
ʾbyḥy	650–625	24(#103), 41a(v.3, p.67), 61(v.2, p.878), 702, 748(A4), 733(#70), 805(p.45), 856(#103), 857(#103).
ʾbndb	625–600	634, 748(A36).
ʾdnplṭ	675–650	24(#98), 42(p.209,343), 698a, 729, 733(#99), 748(A2), 805(p.42), 847, 856(#98), 857(#98), 960.
ʾhʾb	700–600	749(#106).
ʾlʾ	700–650	748(A17), 856(#262), 939.
ʾlybr	650–625	50(p.55), 648(v.3, p.80), 748(A29), 846, 856(#133), 857(#133).
ʾlybr	675–625	648(v.3, p.80), 748(A28).
ʾlyʿm	675–650	24(#6), 42(p.127), 50(p.66), 61(v.3, p.1873), 648(v.1, p.347), 703(#44), 733(#69), 748(A35), 856(#6).
ʾlyšʿ	600–575	679, 748(A6).
ʾlmšl	650–550	678(#35).
ʾlndb	700–675	633(#20), 748(A30).
ʾlndb	700–600	749(#101).
ʾlntn	700–600	778(#34).

158

Index of Ammonite Personal Seals
(unknown provenance)

"seal of..."	Date	Bibliographic Reference Number
ʾlsmky	650-550	50(p.54), 648(v.3, p.80), 748(P11), 805(p.28), 810, 856(#129).
ʾlʿz	625-600	650, 748(A38), 856(#170), 857(#170).
ʾlšgb	625-600	24(#59), 41(r,p.11), 42(p.219), 50(p.69), 714, 733(#46), 748(A7), 771(p.36), 805(p.30), 856(#59).
ʾlšmʿ	700-600	749(#111).
ʾlšmʿ	725-675	631, 748(A26).
ʾlšmʿ	700-600	678(#32).
ʾltmk	700-600	633(#18), 748(A33), 749(#105).
ʾmrʾl	625-600	36a(#135), 748(A8), 749(#104), 857(#259), 939.
bṭš	625-600	748(A31), 779, 788, 856(#221), 857(#221).
bydʾl	725-700	15a(p.76), 678(p.57), 703, 733(#30), 748(A3), 946.
bydʾl	550-450	749(#113).
bqš	650-600	50(p.64), 748(A18), 749(#103), 805(p.38), 812, 856(#159).
gʾdt	?	856(#229), 857(#229), 952a.
hnʾ	700-600	749(#112).
hṭš	700-675	676, 748(A19).

Index of Ammonite Personal Seals
(unknown provenance)

"seal of..."	Date	Bibliographic Reference Number
yš‹	625-600	50(p.60), 646, 648(v.4, p.925), 748(A41), 810, 856(#146).
yš‹›l	625-600	13(pl.9.23), 24(#86), 42(p.291), 50(#71), 56(p.770), 61(v.1, p.57), 714, 733(#29), 748(A34), 856(#86).
kpr	700-600	749(#99).
mkm›l	700-600	749(#107).
mg›nrt	675-625	649a, 748(A9), 846a, 856(#225), 857(#225).
mnḥm	725-675	748(A21), 857(#264).
mnḥm	700-600	678(#33).
mnr	?	678(#36).
mr‹	700-600	748(A27).
mt›	700-600	749(#110).
ndb›l	750-650	678(#29).
ndb›l	700-650	657, 748(All), 788, 856(#201).
ndb›l	675-625	748(A10), 749(#102), 857(#263), 939.
‹bd	675-625	657, 748(All).
‹bd›	700-600	649(pl.44), 748(A44), 788, 856(#217), 857(#217).

160

Index of Ammonite Personal Seals
(unknown provenance)

seal of..."	Date	Bibliographic Reference Number
ʿzrʾ	725-675	749(#97).
ʿmsʾl	725-675	748(A22), 754, 956.
ʿšnʾl	725-700	13(pl.9.24), 24(#88), 42(p.346), 50(#71), 648(v.3, p.80), 724, 733(#21), 748(A39), 771(p.13), 856(#88).
pdʾl	650-600	50(p.56), 648(v.3, p.80), 748(A43), 749(#100), 805(p.40), 811, 856(#135), 857(#135).
plṭ	700-600	678(#31).
šwḥr	700-600?	857(#261).
šwḥr	600-575	36a(#24), 748(A14), 749(#10), 939.
šmʿ	700-600	633(#19), 748(A42).
šmʿ	700-650	633, 748(A40), 749(#88), 805(p.30).
šmʿl	700-675	676, 748(A24).
tmkʾ	700-675	648(v.3, p.80), 678(p.57), 733(#27), 748(A25), 805(p.41).
tmkʾl	700-600	678(#28).
tmkʾl	700-600	678(#30).
tmkʾl	?	678(p.57), 733(#51).
tmkʾl	?	733(#45).
tnr?	?	678(p.57), 733(#26).

161

Index of Edomite Personal Seals

Site	Artifact	"seal of.."	Date	Bibliographic Reference Number
Aroʿer	seal	qwsʾ	650-600	672, 748(E6).
Buseireh	seal	tw	750-700	748(E8), 994.
Buseireh	seal	mlklbʿ	700-650	668, 748(E3), 994.
Buseireh	seal	šmʿʾl	650-600	747, 748(E5).
Tell el-Kheleifeh	impression	qwsʿnl	750-650	570, 572, 573, 748(E4), 856(#119), 857(#119), 865.
Tell el-Kheleifeh	seal	ytm	700-650	35, 50(p.54), 574, 578, 636, 648(v.3, p.622), 733(#39a), 734a, 748(E2), 856(#131), 857(#131).
Umm el-Biyarra (Petra)	impression	qwsq	700-650	748(E1), 856(#227), 857(#227), 882.
Umm el-Biyarra (Petra)	seal	bʿzrʾl	650-600	748(E7), 856(#118), 948.

Index of Moabite Personal Seals

Site	Artifact	"seal of..."	Date	Bibliographic Reference Number
Damascus	seal	kmšyhy	725-675	681a(#2515), 733(#71), 748(M7), 856(#111), 857(#111).
Damascus	seal	mš‛	700-650	576, 748(M6), 749(#115), 788, 856(#114), 857(#114).
el-Kerak	seal	nsr’l	?	24(#102), 61(v.3, p.1267), 856(#102), 993.
Tello (Lagash)	seal	b‛lntn	650-600	24(#81-82), 41a(v.1, p.139), 42(p.241), 61(#1822-3), 714, 733(#91), 737, 748(M8), 766, 856(#81-82).
Ur	seal	kmšntn	625-575	748(M3), 857(#265), 939.
?	seal	’mš	700-650	24(#74), 35, 36a(#16), 42(p.220, 330), 50(p.70), 648(v.1, p.430), 733(#122), 748(M1), 749(#1), 856(#74), 857(#74).
?	seal	hšk	800-700	24(#77), 42(p.281), 631, 714, 748(M9), 771(p.43), 856(#77).
?	seal	kmš	700-600	749(#114).
?	seal	kmšm’š	650-600	748(M2), 857(#266), 939.
?	seal	kmš‛m	725-675	36a(#17), 576, 648(v.3, p.80; v.4, p.187), 748(M4), 749(#2), 788, 805(p.40), 856(#113), 857(#113), 939, 996.
?	seal	kmšṣdq	725-650	61(#1263), 733(#92), 748(M5), 838, 856(#112), 857(#112).
?	seal	mš‛	600-500	646, 749(#116), 810.
?	seal	mšpṭ	600-500	749(#117), 857(#267?), 939.

Index of Authors